CAMBRIDGE LIBRARY COLLECTION

Books of enduring scholarly value

History

The books reissued in this series include accounts of historical events and movements by eye-witnesses and contemporaries, as well as landmark studies that assembled significant source materials or developed new historiographical methods. The series includes work in social, political and military history on a wide range of periods and regions, giving modern scholars ready access to influential publications of the past.

The Manuscripts of Westminster Abbey

Joseph Armitage Robinson (1858–1933) was an internationally regarded scholar of early Christian texts, as well as an influential churchman, theologian, historian and pioneer of Anglican–Catholic ecumenical dialogue. While he was Dean of Westminster, he collaborated with the outstanding medievalist and palaeographer M. R. James, then Provost of King's College, Cambridge, on this study, originally published in 1908. It documents the history of the library at Westminster Abbey and its accompanying scriptorium from 1060 to 1660, the original library having been dispersed at the dissolution of the monasteries and its successor destroyed by a fire in 1694. The authors present surprisingly detailed information, compiled from surviving sources, about the buildings, furniture and holdings of the library, its administration, the budget for buying and restoring books, and acquisitions from gifts and legacies. James even succeeds in identifying some manuscripts once owned by Westminster that have survived in other collections.

Cambridge University Press has long been a pioneer in the reissuing of out-of-print titles from its own backlist, producing digital reprints of books that are still sought after by scholars and students but could not be reprinted economically using traditional technology. The Cambridge Library Collection extends this activity to a wider range of books which are still of importance to researchers and professionals, either for the source material they contain, or as landmarks in the history of their academic discipline.

Drawing from the world-renowned collections in the Cambridge University Library, and guided by the advice of experts in each subject area, Cambridge University Press is using state-of-the-art scanning machines in its own Printing House to capture the content of each book selected for inclusion. The files are processed to give a consistently clear, crisp image, and the books finished to the high quality standard for which the Press is recognised around the world. The latest print-on-demand technology ensures that the books will remain available indefinitely, and that orders for single or multiple copies can quickly be supplied.

The Cambridge Library Collection will bring back to life books of enduring scholarly value (including out-of-copyright works originally issued by other publishers) across a wide range of disciplines in the humanities and social sciences and in science and technology.

The Manuscripts of Westminster Abbey

JOSEPH ARMITAGE ROBINSON
MONTAGUE RHODES JAMES

CAMBRIDGE
UNIVERSITY PRESS

CAMBRIDGE UNIVERSITY PRESS

Cambridge, New York, Melbourne, Madrid, Cape Town, Singapore,
São Paolo, Delhi, Dubai, Tokyo, Mexico City

Published in the United States of America by Cambridge University Press, New York

www.cambridge.org
Information on this title: www.cambridge.org/9781108027878

© in this compilation Cambridge University Press 2011

This edition first published 1908
This digitally printed version 2011

ISBN 978-1-108-02787-8 Paperback

NOTES AND DOCUMENTS

RELATING TO

WESTMINSTER ABBEY

No. 1

THE MANUSCRIPTS OF WESTMINSTER ABBEY

CAMBRIDGE UNIVERSITY PRESS WAREHOUSE,

C. F. CLAY, Manager.

London: FETTER LANE, E.C.

Edinburgh: 100, PRINCES STREET.

Leipzig: F. A. BROCKHAUS.

Berlin: A. ASHER AND CO.

New York: G. P. PUTNAM'S SONS.

Bombay and Calcutta: MACMILLAN AND CO., Ltd.

THE MANUSCRIPTS OF
WESTMINSTER ABBEY

BY

J. ARMITAGE ROBINSON, D.D.

DEAN OF WESTMINSTER

AND

MONTAGUE RHODES JAMES, Litt.D.

PROVOST OF KING'S COLLEGE, CAMBRIDGE

CAMBRIDGE:

AT THE UNIVERSITY PRESS

1908

Cambridge:

PRINTED BY JOHN CLAY, M.A.

AT THE UNIVERSITY PRESS.

PREFACE

THE Library of the Dean and Chapter of Westminster contains now but a small batch of manuscripts, and these have for the most part no connexion with Westminster Abbey. They represent however the last of three quite distinct collections, of which the first was dispersed or destroyed at the dissolution of the monastery, and the second perished by fire in 1694. It so happens that of both these earlier collections a considerable amount of evidence is preserved in various quarters.

The Westminster Muniments contain a good deal of scattered information as to the care of books both in monastic times and in the later period, and this has been drawn together here as a small contribution to the history of the Abbey.

The division of responsibility for this little book is indicated by the initials in the table of contents. The Dean and Chapter are under a great obligation to the Provost of King's for having placed his unrivalled experience in these matters at their disposal. They hope that this may be the first of a series of studies which bear on the history of the Church of which it is their high privilege to be the guardians.

J. ARMITAGE ROBINSON.

CONTENTS

I.

ON THE MAKING AND KEEPING
OF BOOKS IN WESTMINSTER ABBEY,

A.D. 1160—1660.

1.

In the chapter house at Westminster there is exhibited a document in which Abbot Gervase and the Convent assign a sum of eight shillings a year from the tithes of Rothing to the Precentor, for the repair of books in the library and for other requirements of his office.

Gervasius abbas beati Petri Westmonasteriensis totusque conventus ejusdem ecclesiae omnibus hominibus suis tam praesentibus quam futuris salutem. Manifestum vobis fieri volumus nos amore dei pro reparandis libris armarii, et pro ceteris negotiis quae ad cantoris nostri pertine[n]t officium, communi assensu et consilio concessisse et dedisse cantariae .viii. solidos de decima de Roinges quam tenet Aluricus presbiter : et his terminis, ad annuntiationem sanctae Mariae .iiii. solidos, et ad festivitatem Sancti Petri ad vincula .iiii. solidos. Quapropter volumus et praecipimus ut cantor ecclesiae beati Petri Westmonasteriensis, quisquis ille fuerit, praedictos habeat solidos bene et honorifice et in pace, ne quis eum super hac nostra donatione et praedicta elemosina ullo modo inquietet[1].

Gervase was Abbot from 1140 to about 1159. Accordingly we see that in the twelfth century the books of the monastery at Westminster were under the charge of the Precentor. This was in accordance with the Constitutions drawn up for all Benedictine monasteries in England by Lanfranc at the end of the eleventh century. In his chapter *De Cantore* we read:

De universis monasterii libris curam gerat, et eos in custodia sua habeat, si ejus studii et scientiae sit ut eorum custodia ei commendari debeat[2].

[1] *Munim.* 1172 A: a copy is in the Westminster 'Domesday,' f. 679*b*, among 'Scripta vacua nunc.' The annual payment of 8*s*. from the rector of Rothing Alba [White Roothing, co. Essex] was surrendered in 1300 (*Munim.* 1172 B, 'Domesday,' f. 360).

[2] Reyner, *Apostolatus Benedictinorum in Anglia*, 1626, append. p. 236: Wilkins, *Concilia*, 1737, I 348.

These words are embodied in the Customary of Westminster, begun under Abbot Ware in 1266[1]. Here we read, on p. 36 of the published edition:

Qui similiter incaustum fieri faciet, quociens opus fuerit; et illud non solummodo fratribus, sed eciam secularibus petentibus curialiter impendet. Atque fratrum necessitatibus de membrana providere tenetur; atque scripta in capitulo legenda legere, componenda componere, corrigenda corrigere, atque sigillanda sigillare. Cujus eciam specialiter incumbit officio unius clavis de cista in qua commune sigillum et privilegia reconduntur per conventum custodiam habere. .

Thus we see that the Precentor has a general responsibility in regard to all matters of writing; and he has to provide ink and parchment. In the next sentence the words adopted from Lanfranc are italicised:

Et insuper *de universis* armariorum *libris curam geret, et eos in custodia habebit,* sed [l. *si] ejus studii et scientiae* est *ut eorum custodia ei* competenter *debeat commendari.* Omnes vero libros qui in sua et succentoris custodia sunt, tam in ecclesia quam in claustro, necnon libros necessarios ac antiphonarios qui magistri noviciorum curae commendantur, renovare, ligare, et quociens opus fuerit sumptibus suis resarcire faciet; ita tamen, si scriptores teneat, quod de eorum victui necessariis per conventum aliquantulum subveniatur eidem.

In earlier days these duties did not ordinarily take the Precentor beyond the cloister, where writing was doubtless done in the carrels of the north walk. But by this time a special Scriptorium had been provided (p. 97):

Quoniam olim ipsi proculdubio precentori non licebat absque licencia a claustro egredi, usque ad tempus illud quo primum facta est domus scriptoriae, nisi solummodo ad sartoriam, ad incaustum faciendum cum opus fuisset.... Sed, a tempore quo constructa est domus prelibata, permissum est ei infra septa monasterii non petita licencia quaquaversum incedere.

This special function of the Precentor is illustrated by the fact that at a later date the Registers, which contain copies of documents which have passed the convent seal, bear his name. Thus the first part of Register A, which begins with the first year of K. Henry VII, was written 'tempore administrationis fratris Johannis Watyrden in officio Precentoris.'

---

[1] The Customary contains passages written after the death of K. Henry III (1272). It has been edited for the Henry Bradshaw Society by Sir E. Maunde Thompson, together with the derived Customary of St Augustine's, Canterbury. By the aid of the latter the Westminster MS. (now Cotton. Otho C xi), which suffered severely in the Ashburnham House fire of 1731, has been largely restored. The editor had made a transcript of it for the Dean and Chapter in 1867, and this contains a considerable portion which, owing to its fragmentary condition, was not included in the published volume.

The Precentor's responsibility for church books was shared by the Succentor (p. 37):

Ad succentoris specialiter pertinet officium bibliam magni voluminis atque libros officio chori necessarios custodire et in chorum portare quociens opus fuerit, ac iterato salvo reponere.

The Sacrist had the responsibility, in concert with the Precentor, of providing and repairing missals and altar-books in general (p. 49).

The Precentor at Westminster bore also the title of *Armarius*. Whereas Lanfranc's chapter relating to his office begins with the words:

Cantor, quamdiu Abbas in monasterio est...

the Westminster Customary says:

Cantor, qui et alio nomine Armarius appellatur, eo quod de libris curam habere solet qui in armariis continentur, *quamdiu Abbas in monasterio est*...[1].

This title of Armarius carries us on to consider the place where the books were kept. There can be no doubt that here, as at Durham, there were 'almeries of wainscot' (*armaria*, cupboards for books) in the north walk of the cloister against the wall of the church[2]; the carrels, or wooden enclosures forming diminutive studies for the monks, being opposite against the traceried arches, which at one time were at least partially glazed[3].

The following references to the *carolae* and *armaria* may be quoted from the Customary:

De carolis vero in claustro habendis hanc consideracionem habere debent, quibus committitur claustri tutela, ut videlicet celerarius forinsecus aut intrinsecus, vel infirmarius, aut camerarius, seu alii fratres qui raro in claustro resident, suas carolas in claustro non habeant; sed neque aliqui fratres, nisi in scribendo, vel

---

[1] P. 28. The inserted clause was carried into the Canterbury Customary (p. 90), though the regulations which follow are very different.

[2] *Rites of Durham*, Surtees Society, 1903, p. 83. See J. W. Clark, *On Libraries at Lincoln, Westminster and St Paul's*, Camb. Antiq. Soc. Proceedings, vol. ix (18 Feb. 1895), and *Care of Books*, 1901, pp. 91 ff., where traces of the *armaria*, as detected by Micklethwaite, are noted. The suggestion that the absence of shafts in the northernmost bay of the wall arcade in the east cloister walk was designed to leave room for the *armarium commune* is rendered improbable by the fact that the Customary assigns this place for the Abbot's seat in the cloister (p. 157), 'in capite partis orientis claustri': next was the prior's place 'in aquilonari parte, juxta hostium ecclesiae': no one else had a seat specially appropriated except the master of the novices, who was at the extreme west, and the brother 'cui committitur armariorum claustri custodia.'

[3] In *Munim.* 24,855 is an estimate for repairing the glass in the cloisters, *temp.* Commonwealth. H. Keepe (*Monumenta Westm.*, p. 177) writes in 1683: 'on every side opposite to the Walls (where now are only frames of wood) was fine glazed Windows of tinctured glass of divers colours.'

illuminando, aut tantum notando, communitati aut eciam sibimet ipsis proficere sciant (p. 165).

Quos [sc. novicios] cum viderit magister eorum perfecte scire quae scire debent, consuevit eis dicere ut in alia parte sedeant, loco talibus assignato, ubi tunc licite possunt libros de armariis seniorum respicere; sed nondum scribere aut carolas habere debent, licet fuerint sacerdotes, nisi viderit magister quod eorum scriptura ecclesiae possit proficere (p. 168).

It was the custom on a certain day in Lent to produce and redistribute books in the chapter house. An allusion to this occurs on p. 90: 'die qua in capitulo legitur leccio de Quadragesimae observacione et codices ostenduntur.' This is borne out by a Canterbury regulation (p. 39): ' die videlicet qua fratres secundum regulam de bibliotheca, id est librario, sunt in capitulo codices accepturi': on that day a mass was to be said for benefactors of the library. The custom is fully described in Lanfranc's Constitutions (Reyner, append. 216; Wilkins I 332 f.).

The following documents will serve to illustrate the cost of books and the manner of their production in the fourteenth and fifteenth centuries.

I. In 1376 Simon Langham died at Avignon. Seven chests of books came to Westminster as part of his legacy to the Abbey. They were valued before they were committed to the merchants who undertook to transmit them as far as Bruges. The valuation is preserved in a mutilated form in *Munim.* 9,226, of which *Munim.* 9,225 is an early and complete (though often inaccurate) copy. I give it here from the original, using the copy to fill up gaps[1]:

Estimacio librorum bone memorie dñi Cardinalis Cant'.

Prima Cista.

Inprimis dictionarius in tribus voluminibus	ii^{c} fr.
Item .iiii. Ewangelia Glosata in uno volumine	xv fr.
5 Item summa Valent'	ii fr.
Item constituciones benedictini cum aliis	viii s.

Summa ii^{c} xvii fr. viii s.

Secunda.

Item Gregorius super Ezechielem	iii fr.
10 Item Ricardus de media villa	viii fr.
Item quodlibet Hervei	iii fr.
Item quedam facta circa ordinem Monachorum per beatum Bernardum in parvo volumine	i fr.
Item actus et exilium sancte Thome in quaternis · creditur esse cant'	ii fr.

---

[1] This document is copied from *Munim.* 9,225 into *Liber Niger Quaternus* (f. 146 b ff.), but somewhat carelessly.

15 Item repertorium de paupere de materia indulgenciarum   di. fr.
Item Ultima pars summe sancte Thome sine asseribus   iii fr.
Item Grisostimus super Matheum cum aliis parvis scriptis   vi fr.
Item Lira super .iiii. ewangelia et Epistolas Pauli   xxxvii fr. et di.
Item Milleloquium Augustini   xx iiii fr.
20 Item quedam tabula de diversis doctoribus   ii fr.
Item temata divisa per alphabetum cum una tabula in fine   iii fr.
Item diversa Originalia Agustini · quindecim in uno volumine   xii fr.
Item tabula Berengarii super Speculum   xiii fr.
Item Augustinus super psalterium abbreviatus cum septem quaternis
25   non ligatis   i fr.
Item tercia pars lire continens ysaiam · Jeremiam · trenorum · daniel ·
Makabeorum · xii prophete minores · baruk · Ezechiel   xxxvii fr. et di.

Summa ii$\overset{c}{}$ xii fr. et di.

Tercia.
30 Item lewes super iiii^{or} sentenciarum   xii fr.
Item sermones borage   vi fr.
Item originale Agustini de trinitate cum aliis   xii fr.
Item prima pars et secunda pars Thome super Ewangelia in ii^{bus}
voluminibus   xx fr.
35 Item gregorius in pastoralibus et exameron ambrozii sine asseribus   ii fr.
Item passio sancte Thome cum epistolis suis et privatus sancti gregorii   i fr.
Item secundum volumen lire continens esdras · nemias · ester · Job ·
tobias · judit · psalterium · proverbia · ecclesiastes · cantica ·
40   sapiencia · ecclesiasticus   xxxvii fr. et di.
Item armakanus de questionibus armenorum cum sermonibus suis   xxx fr.
Item par decretalium   xxii fr.
Item Bi[b]lia in parvo volumine   xii fr.
Item de claustro anime   iiii fr.
45 Item libre beati bernardi   xii fr.
Item distinctiones malicii   ii fr.

Summa clx[x]ii fr. et di.
Quarta.
Item Innocencius super Decretales   xii fr.
50 Item Egidius de regimine principum   iiii fr.
Item parve concordancie   i fr.
Item de exemplis scripturarum sacrarum   ii fr.
Item Speculum Historiale prima pars   l fr.
Item Augustinus de Civitate dei   xii fr.
55 Item de proprietatibus rerum   vi fr.
Item decreta   xx fr.
Item dealogus Gregorii   iiii fr.
Item Johannes Calderini et unus tractatus continens de paupere contra
prophesias [Johannis] de Rapecisa   i fr.
60 Item Thomas de Veritate   vi fr.
Item epistole Pauli glosate   xvi fr.
Item Josue · Judit · esdras · makabeorum cum aliis   xii fr.

Summa cxlvi fr.

Quinta.

65 Item Tabula sermonum sancti Augustini cum armakanis de pauperie
salvatoris   iiii fr.
Item Thomas de equino super de anima   ii fr.
Item primum volumen de lira   xxxvii fr. et di.
Item Thomas super primum sentenciarum   iii fr.
70 Item lira moralizans totam bibliam   xxx fr.
1tem Marcus et Matheus glosati   vi fr.
Item Ezechiel et daniel glosati   viii fr.
Item Jenesis et exodus glosati   viii fr.
Item Regum et parolipominon glosati   viii fr.
75 Item Leviticus · numerum · deuteronomii glosati   viii fr.
Item concordancie bib[l]ie   xv fr.
Item tercium et quartum scriptum durandi   vi s.
Item vita sancte Thome monachi et Martiris doverre   vi s.
Item quaterni de propheciis   vi s.
80   Summa clv fr. vi s. [cxxxv fr. et di *in copy*].

Sexta.

Item prima pars summe sancte Thome   iii fr.
Item Hugo super Johannem et super aliis monasterii Grandcourt de
Flandria   iiii fr.
Item sentencie Petri Lumbardi   vi fr.
85 Item Thomas super quartum Sentenciarum   vi fr.
Item Epistole sancti Augustini   viii fr.
Item Boicius de consolacione philosophie cum aliis   x fr.
Item Thomas super libros phisicorum   iii fr.
Item Thomas super librum metaphisice   iii fr.
90 Item secunda pars summe sancte Thome   vi fr.
Item summa contra gentiles   vi fr.
Item tabula originalium   xx fr.
Item libri Ancelmi   viii fr.
Item ysaias · Jeremias · trenorum glosati   vi fr.
95 Item · xl · quaterni · Ba[r]tholomei · Jacobi · berengarii involuti in duobus
manutergiis que sunt Thome de Southam   xvi fr.

                              Summa cv fr.

Septima.

Item Summa hostiensis   xx fr.
100 Item liber sextus cum clementinis et cum glosis   xvi fr.
Item liber salamonis glosatus   vi fr.
Item Thomas super secundum sentenciarum   vi fr.
Item Thomas super tercium sentenciarum   vi fr.
Item unum mariale   iiii fr.
105 Item psalterium glosatum   xii fr.
Item xii prophete parvi glosati   iiii fr.
Item registrum gregorii   ii fr.
Item liber de concideracione sancti bernardi cum aliis   iii fr.
Item historia ecclesiastica · creditur Cristi Cant'   viii fr.
110 Item cronica martiniana · Beda de gestis Anglorum et vita sancte
Thome in uno volumine   x fr.

Item Thomas de malo	vi fr.
Item de potencia dei	iiii fr.
Item excepciones librorum beati gregorii	ii fr.
115 Item ancelmus de Similitudinibus	ii fr.
Item exposicio super ester et Judit	ii fr.

Summa cxiii fr.

Dr James gives me the following notes on some of the books and writers mentioned in the above list:

- l. 5. Valent' (*or* Valenc'). Is this for Faventini or Placentini? or Wallensis?
- 6. Benedictini] *lege* Benedictinae.
- 10. Ricardus de media villa. Author of *quaestiones* on the Sentences, &c.
- 11. Herveus Natalis Brito, author of *Quodlibeta*.
- 14. Thought to belong to Christ Church, Canterbury: cf. l. 109. The form 'sancte Thome' regularly recurs in this list.
- 19. An anthology of St Augustine by Bartholomew of Urbino.
- 23. Berengarii super Speculum. Berengarius Fredolis, Bp of Beziers.
- 31. Sermones Borage. ? Simon Boraston or Jac. de Voragine.
- 35. sine asseribus] without boards: probably in a vellum wrapper.
- 41. Richard Fitzralph, Abp of Armagh. This book seems to have been seen by Leland, see below, p. 23.
- 44. de Claustro anime. By Hugo de Folieto.
- 46. Malicii] probably for Mauricii.
- 53. Speculum Historiale. By Vincent 'of Beauvais.'
- 55. de proprietatibus rerum. By Barth. Anglicus.
- 57. dealogus] dialogus.
- 58. Johannes Calderini of Bologna, Doctor of Canon Law, wrote a Commentary on the Decretals.
- 59. [Johannis] de Rapecisa. John de Rupescissa (Rochetaillade), Minorite: his prophecy is in Browne's *Fasciculus*.
- 78. Thomas, monk and martyr of Dover: Thomas de la Hale, killed by the French at Dover in 1295.
- 83. Probably Hugo de Sancto Caro, otherwise called Hugo de Vienna. Monasterii Grandcourt (*ut videtur*)?
- 104. There was a *Mariale* (a work on the glories of the Virgin) by Albertus Magnus. Also one by Jac. de Voragine.
- 110. Cronica Martiniana. By Martinus Polonus.

II. The cost of making Abbot Litlington's Missal: from the Abbot's Treasurer's roll for 1383–4[1].

Expense noui Missalis [*in margin*].

In xiij. duodenis percamenti vitulini emptis pro vno nouo missali faciendo iiij. li. vj. s. viij. d.

Et in illuminacione grossarum litterarum xxij.ˡⁱ iii.ᵈ

---

[1] This has been printed on a loose slip as an *addendum* to the third fasciculus of the Westminster Missal by its editor, Dr J. Wickham Legg. Similar accounts are printed, from St George's, Windsor, by J. H. Middleton, *Illuminated MSS.*, p. 220; and by G. G. Gray, *Early Cambridge Stationers*, pp. 18 ff.

Et pro ligacione dicti missalis .xxj.s.
Et .j. homini scribenti notas in dicto missali iij.s. iiij.^{d}
Et pro coopertura dicti missalis .viij.s. iiij.^{d}
Et pro broudura eiusdem vj.s. x.d.
Et pro registro eiusdem missalis xx.d.
Et pro pictura dicti missalis x.s.
In vj. nodulis emptis pro eodem xij.s.
In j. baga empta pro eodem iiij.^{s} vj.^{d}
Et in feodo Thome Preston per duos annos scribentis dictum missale iiij.li.
In panno empto pro liberatura dicti Thome per dictum tempus xx.s.

Summa xxxiiij.li. xiiij.s. vij.d.

Thomas Preston received a fee and cloth of livery during the two years in which he was occupied upon the book; moreover in the Abbot's Treasurer's roll for 1382–3 we read of a payment to Fr. W. Warfeld 'pro mensa Thome Preston commorantis secum ad mensam' from St John Baptist's Day to Advent (*sic*), viz. 26 weeks, 21/8. It is clear therefore that he was not a monk. But it is interesting to note that in 1384–5 there was a novice named Thomas Preston, who sang his first mass in 1386–7, and appears in the Chamberlain's roll as late as 1420. May we not identify this monk with the former scrivener?

III. The Infirmarer's roll for 1386–7 contains the following entries:

Et in tribus .xii. de velym emp pro nouo Missali .xxi.s. precio .xii. vii.s. Et pro rasura .xiiii. quaternorum dicti Missalis .ii.s. iiii.d. Et pro vermilon et incausto .xviii.d. Et in azuro pro Kalendar' .vi.d. Et solut' Thome Rolf pro illuminacione & ligamine Missalis predicti .lxx.s. xi.d.

Et solut' pro coopertura Portoforii quondam Nichi Abbatis et ex dono eiusdem Capelle Infirmarie .vii.s. vi.d.

The Infirmarer had not to pay for the writing of his missal. Perhaps it was written by the new monk Thomas Preston[1].

---

[1] A few items of the same period may be added here:

(1) 1369. *Liber Niger Quat.* f. 79. *De libris accommodatis per Abbatem Archidiacono Oxon. etc.* Anno domini millesimo ccclxix^{no} et regni regis Edwardi tercii...primo die Augusti facte sunt indenture inter Abbatem et Conventum Westm' et Magistrum Thomam Southam Arch' Oxon' de libris accomodatis dicto magistro Thome ad terminum xx.^{ti} annorum proxime sequent' · videlicet: Decretal' coopert' cum viridi. Item prima pars Johannis in Novell' super Decretal'. Item secunda pars Novelle cum quodam prologo bublie. Item liber Decretorum. Item Archidiaconus in Rosario super Decreta.

(2) 1371–2. Abbot's Household (R. Fortheye, Clerk of Kitchen): 50^s paid 'pro emendacione unius magni missalis et unius parui missalis de Capella dñi.'

(3) 1384–5. Abbot's Treasurer: 3^s 2^d for covering a great Portiforium; 5^s 8^d for covering a book and making three silver clasps.

(4) 1388–9. Sacrist: 'pro libro registri de vestibulo x^s.' This is the Inventory of the Vestry (now at Canterbury) which has been edited by Dr Wickham Legg (*Archaeologia*, LII, 1890).

IV. In the *Liber Niger Quaternus* (f. 92) we have the following entry (A.D. 1398–9):

Memorandum de Expensis factis pro factura magni novi libri in medio chori, anno regni regis Ricardi secundi xxii^{do}.

In primis R. Hermod' solvit pro uno quaterno pleno totaliter, tam pro velym quam scriptura et illuminacione.

Item Dn̄s W. Colchester Abbas solvit vi^s viii^d. Dn̄s J. Godmerston vi^s viii^d. Radulphus Tonworth vi^s viii^d. Johannes Crendon xx^d. Robertus Watele xx^d. Willelmus Amodesham xii^d. Elminus Merston totum librum notavit absque precio. Edwardus Whaddon solvit xx^d.

Isti supradicti solverunt, et nullus alius de conventu. Eodem anno Johannes Kingeston fuit Ultimus in congregacione.

Item eodem anno pro eodem libro, praeter quaternum quem fecit frater R. Hermod', Radulphus Tonworth de pecunia predicta solvit pro v dosen de velym et una pelle, precii duodene vi^s—xxviii^s vi^d. Item pro scriptura solutum Johanni Heruynton xxv^s ii^d. Item pro biys vermylon et opere illuminatoris xxxiii^s iiii^d. Item solutum Johanni Fouler pro illuminatione vi^s viii^d.

Summa ………

Abbot Colchester succeeded Litlyngton in 1486. Of the other subscribers we may note that Robert Whately was Prior in 1407, and William Agmondesham was Archdeacon in 1414. Robert Hermondsworth[1] was the Keeper of the Lady Chapel who granted the lease of a house to Geoffrey Chaucer in 1399 (*Munim.* Chapt. House no. lvii). John Hervynton (or Hernynton) was doubtless a hired scribe, and John Fowler a hired illuminator : but the musical notation was done at home. 'Bice' is a brown pigment, and in Murray's *Dictionary* we have the similar combinations, 'bis azur,' 'bis vert,' &c.

V. The next example is a century later, and in English : *Munim.* 9326, a paper roll with contributions on one side and payments on the other : the date is c. 1492.

Payments for the newe repairyng of the Seyny bookes.

G. Fassett priour payeth for the byndyng of the ii bookes.

Th. Arundell	
J. Ramsey	xx^d
W. Wycome	
W. Lambart	
J. Hampton	iii^s iiii^d
R. Charyng	iii^s iiii^d
J. Waterdene	iii^s iiii^d

[1] A monk named H. de Hermod' died in 1392; and another named Robert de Hermodesworth gives an account of the property of his sister, Alice Sakvill, in 1444 (Widmore, *Cat.* pp. 126 A, and 102). Harmondsworth, co. Middlesex, near Staines, appears as *Heremodesworde* in Domesday.

J. Drope	iii^s iiii^d
W. Brewode	iiii^s
R. Langley	ii^s
W. Grawnte	iii^s iiii^d
J. Holonde	iii^s iiii^d

Th. Flete paieth for the stuff that shall belong to the bookes, and also gevith the writer of them his borde.

T. Elie	iii^s iiii^d
R. Newbery	iii^s iiii^d
J. Norton	ii^s
R. Caston	ii^s

W. Lokynton paieth for the peecyng of the bokes. And also fyndith the writer his bedd.

W. Mane	iii^s iiii^d
J. Islip	
T. Barkar	x^s
J. Brice	iii^s iiii^d
J. Assheley	iii^s iiii^d
T. Champeney	
W. Redyng	
H. Jonys	iii^s iiii^d
J. Warde	iii^s iiii^d
W. Grove	
T. Salle	ii^s
J. Albon	iii^s iiii^d
T. Browne	iii^s iiii^d
R. Humfrey	iii^s iiii^d
W. Grene	ii^s
Ch. Chamber	ii^s
R^o. Davers	ii^s
M. James	iii^s iiii^d
J. Redemayne	ii^s
R^a. Worsley	ii^s
R^a. Romney	ii^s
W. Southwell	ii^s

Sum in expences is a c^s ii^s x^d
Sum Received is iiii^{lb} xiiii^s iiii^d
Sum to Receive is viii^s ii^d

On the verso:

Thies be the costes that be leyde owte for the Seyny books.

In primis for lymnyng of the oon boke in grete letters. c et dim.⎫ price of the hunderd x^d . . . . ⎭	xv^d
Item for iiii^c Smale letters and xxiiii. price per c. v^d . . .	xxii^d
Item paide for ii Bukkys Skynnys	iiii^s
Item paid for iiii Clapsis. and xx bullions	viii^s
Item paide for lether and grete wyer for them	xv^d
Item for iii White Skynnes	xii^d
Item for iiii Rede Skynnes	xx^d

Item paide for the lockes and Cheynes	iiii^s
Item for repairyng of the pewe	viii^s iiii^d
Item paide for oon of the Bookes wrytyng	xxvi^s viii^d
Item paide for new henges and Changyng of the lokkes and also for nailles to them	ii^s iiii^d
Item for the wrytyng of the nexte boke	xxvi^s viii^d
Item for the Florishyng of grete letters. and for the lymnyng of grete letters and smale	xiiii^s iiii^d

Summa c^s

George Fascet was Prior from 1491 till 1498, when he was elected Abbot. A comparison of the lists of monks contained in the Chamberlains' rolls suggests that this document was written about 1492.

But what are the Seyny books? At Worcester we hear of 'seny money,' and at Lincoln of 'seny days.' The word is derived from *sanguinati*, through the French *saignées*. In the Accounts of Worcester Priory, edited by Canon J. M. Wilson, we find (p. 21): 'Et solutum eidem domino priori et conventui pro eorum minucionibus, cum duplicibus dicti domini prioris, vocat. senymoney per annum, 58s. 8d.' 'Seny days' are mentioned in the Customs of Lincoln, edited by Bradshaw and Wordsworth (*Lincoln Statutes* II 575): 'diebus autem nuncupatis Seny days'; cf. cxvii, 164 'De le seyneis' (as a heading), 324 'Poterit seney' (marginal note). They were days of permitted absence during the 'great residence' of Canons: the context of the reference last quoted speaks of blood-letting as a special cause of absence. Again, the monks of Evesham had a house for convalescents at Badsey, which was granted to Sir Philip Hoby in 1545 under the name of the 'seyne house[1].'

The term 'Seyny books' still calls for explanation: and fortunately we find what we want in the Westminster Customary of the thirteenth century. At Westminster, it appears, the monks who had been bled were allowed to sit during certain of the choir services in front of the altar of St Benedict, using a book called the 'liber minutorum.' See, for example, Customary p. 43, 'ad librum vero minutorum unam qualibet nocte ponet candelam (sacrista)'; p. 49, the Sacrist must provide and repair various service books, including 'librum minutorum'; p. 239, 'sanguinati ac ceteri extra chorum existentes, qui pro recta consuetudine, quando vesperae in choro canuntur, ante altare beati Benedicti ad librum sedent minutorum,' cf. p. 240; so again p. 242, 'ad librum minutorum letaniam omnes pariter cum devocione explebunt'; p. 243, 'eosdem psalmos ad librum minutorum ante altare beati

[1] See *Victoria Co. Hist.*, Worcestershire, II 354, where a picture of the house is given.

Benedicti per se dicturus.' At St Augustine's Canterbury there probably was no such 'Seyny book'; for though its recension of the Customary retains the words in the two former references, which come incidentally in the description of the Sacrist's duties, yet in the later passages it drops out the phrase substituting in one case ' *the cross before St Benedict's altar.'*

'The Florishyng of grete letters' might have been done without outside help a few years earlier, as may be seen from the following letter which is appended to the formal *dimissio* of brother Edward Butler, who had sought leave to join the Cluniac brethren of St Milburga's Priory (at Wenlock) in the diocese of Hereford. The letter is sent from Abbot Esteney to Prior Richard Synger (*Register* A f. 30*b*) in April 1489.

Reverent brother in Crist, We grete you wele. And it is so that one Edward Botiller a brother of ours hath often and diverse tymes praied and desired us licence to be dimissed out of our obedience, and he desireth to be a brother of your place and your obedience, and hath grete desire to be with you and in that Contree ; at which desire we have licenced the same Edward and geven hym a dimissyon under our seale. The same Edward hath competent lernyng and understondyng, and can syng bothe playn song and prikked song ; and also a faire writer, a fflorissher and maker of capitall letters. Wherfor I pray you that ye will admitte the same Edward Botiller to be a brother of your place and under your Rule and obedience. And god preserve you. Writen at our Monastery of West^r the ix day of Aprill.

2.

We now pass to the modern period. At the dissolution of the monastery an Inventory was taken—probably in 1541, for the new Bishop had already entered into possession of the Abbot's House[1]. A few church books are included, but the Library is not mentioned. But in the reign of K. Edward VI an Order in Council was made, under Dudley, Earl of Warwick, for 'purging the Library of Westminster of all missals, legends, and other superstitious volumes, and delivering their garniture to Sir Anthony Aucher[2].'

[1] Public Record Office: Land Revenue, Misc. Bks. no. 110: printed in large part by M. E. C. Walcott in *Trans. of Lond. and Middl. Archaeol. Soc.*, Aug. 1873, vol. IV, pt iii.

[2] Quoted by Neale and Brayley I 297 from Collier's *Eccl. Hist.* II 307. The actual Order, passed on 25 Feb. 1550/1, was this: 'The Kinges Majesties lettre ——— for the purging of his Highnes Librarie at Westminster of all superstitiouse bookes, as masse bookes, legendes and suche like, and to deliver the garnyture of the same bookes, being either of golde or silver, to Sir Anthony Aucher in the presence of Sir Thomas Darcie, &c.' But it may be doubted whether this refers to the Abbey Library, which perhaps had already been destroyed, and which would not be likely to contain church books with precious bindings.

A new start was made towards the close of Dean Benson's time. For in the first Chapter Book we read (f. 48):

(13 Jan. 1549.) Also yt is lykwyse determened that the tow lecternes of latten and candelstyckes of latten wythe the angelles of copper and gylte, and all other brasse latten belle mettell and brasse shalbe solde by M^r heynes Treasourer, by cause they be monymentes of Idolatrie and Supersticyon, and the monye thereof cummyng to be receyvyd by the sayd Treasaurer for makyng of the lybrary and bying of bookes for the same.

And it is also agreed that M^r pekyns and M^r keble shall see the weyght of all the sayd metalle ; and that the lybrary shalbe fynisshed in the northe parte of the cloyster, as sone as the money can be made of the premisses.

Up to this point, then, the locality of the Library remains the same. When the monks returned in 1556 the *armaria* were doubtless cleared of their Protestant contents, even if they had escaped the attention of the Marian Dean, Hugh Weston.

Dean Bill (1560) in his draft of Statutes (which is largely based on the Statutes given in 1552 to Trinity College, Cambridge, of which he was Master) contemplates the foundation of a Library. In the Statute *De custodia bonorum collegii*[1] we read :

Si qui libros e bibliotheca, aut quid aliud bonorum collegii, mutuantur, iidem in prodecani commentariis nomen suum subscribant, et de praestatione promittant : qui non praestiterit, vel duplum solvat vel collegio excludatur.

Bibliotheca munda servetur, et alternis diebus scopis mundetur. Huic decanus et capitulum aliquem e ministris assignent, qui eam bene asservandam curet [cui pro labore viginti solidos collegium solvat][2].

Collegium viginti solidos in libris emendis et in bibliotheca collocandis quotannis pendat.

Si quis quid bibliothecae dederit, nomen ejus non modo in principio libri inscribatur, sed etiam tabulae in bibliotheca affigantur, quae omnia donatorum nomina, dona et tempus donationis complectantur.

In 1574 Dean Goodman (1561–1601) inaugurated a new Library with the gift of the Complutensian Bible[3] and a Hebrew vocabulary. In 1st Chap. Bk f. 157, we find this entry:

Bokes given to the College.

M^d that Mr Gabriell Goodman, dean of this Collegiate Churche, the ii^{de} of decembr 1574 gave unto this College towardes a Librarie to be made in the same : Thole Bible secundum Complutensem editionem, conteyned in Five tomes or volumes, and one hebrue vocabulare.

---

[1] Cap. 35 in the Trinity Statutes of 1552.

[2] The words in brackets were inserted later.

[3] Dean Vincent, in his Note-book preserved in the Deanery, says: 'it was imperfect, but was completed by the care of W. V. 1812.'

The work of fitting up a Library was put in hand without delay. An account rendered by Thomas Fowler, surveyor, for six weeks ending 2 April 1575, contains the following passages (*Munim.* 39,037):

Chardges done in making of a newe Liberarye.

Joyners occupied in makinge of a new Liberary in the Colledge of Westminster with other thinges nedefull there to be done, &c.

[Wages, boards, nails, glass.]

Ironworke. To William Conan Smythe for these Parcels followinge, viz. for a paier of Henges and a paier of hookes for a dore in the Liberarye, weyenge vii^{li} at iii^d the pound—xxi^d: for making an upright and a Locket for the tower in the Cloyster where the Liberarye shalbe of their owne stoffe weyenge xi pounde at ii^d the pounde—xxii^d: for making di. [i.e. half] a bitt for a plate Locke in the Liberarye—vi^d: for making a dowble Casemente for the Liberarie—v^s.

....

The Chardges of the Liberarye cometh to the some of—xi^{li} viii^s x^d.

In a similar account, for fourteen weeks ending 9 July 1575 (*Munim.* 39,038), we find:

For making a table in the Liberarie—xvi^s: for making a peace of selling [i.e. panelling] in the Liberary cont. vii yardes and a halfe at ii^s the yarde—xv^s: for iiii joyne stooles in the Liber. at xvi^d the peece—v^s iiii^d.

....

For a dowble stocke locke and a keye for the same Locke for a dore in the Liberarie—iii^s: for another dowble stocke loce for a dore in the Liberarie—ii iiii^d: for a crampyn for the same dore and for yoking it into the walle—vi^d: for ii boultes for the same dore at vi^d the pece—xii^d.

We learn from the former of these accounts that the books were not to be kept (as in the old monastic days and in the time of K. Edward VI) in the north walk of the cloister, but in ' the tower in the Cloyster.' What does this mean ?

Fortunately we are able to answer this question by means of an incidental clause in a lease of 1606, which points to the house over the east cloister, reached from the east walk of the cloister by the turret-staircase. This house is now entirely gone : the last remains of it were the two chambers which till a few years ago blocked up the south part of the Muniment Room. Under the great round arch outside the Muniment Room can still be seen the holes for the beams which carried a floor. The history of the house, so far as it can at present be traced, is as follows : it was (1) a prebendary's house, (2) a Library and an Armoury, (3) let to Thomas Griffin and Thomas Goodman, (4) recovered for the use of a prebendary, (5) let to Colonel Humphreyes under the Commonwealth, (6) let to Bradshawe and largely repaired by him, (7) occupied again by prebendaries until it was pulled down at the time of Wren's restorations in 1711. It is with the earlier of these stages that we are here concerned.

On 4 Dec. 1606 the Chapter Book records (f. 289 *b*):

> A lease to Robert Knowles in trust for the evictinge of Thomas Griffins and Thomas Goodmans lease of the prebendes Lodginge over the Easte cloyster.

The lease, which was sealed next day, specifies (*Munim.* 18,313):

> all those Lodginges, Romthes and Chambers scituate, lyinge and beinge over the East Cloyster on the Sowth side of the said Collegiate Churche, sometimes the Howse and Lodginge belonginge to one of the Prebendes of the said Collegiate Churche, whereof some parte was some tyme ymployed for a library, And some other parte for an Armorie[1] for the said Collegiate Churche, and nowe in the occupation of Thomas Griffine of Westminster.

The lease in dispute had been granted to Thomas Griffin and Thomas Goodman on 6 Dec. 1597. By that date, if not before, the Library must have found a new home: but it is clear that for some years after 1575 it was lodged in a portion of this house.

To this period of its history the following notices belong:

> (*Munim.* 30,392. A.D. 1576.) For a Curten of buckrom to hang afore a Mappe in the Liberarye—iii^s iiii^d.
> For making a Curten Rode and two hookes for a Mappe in the new Liberary being vi foote Longe—xvi^d.
> Cf. *Munim.* 39,389 (earlier in the same year): For a frame for a Mappe—vi^s.
> (*Munim.* 40,192. A.D. 1588.) A Brickleyer and Tylor occupied in Tyling over the Lyberary in the great Cloystre.

In the twelve years which passed after its establishment over the east cloister, the Library had grown, chiefly, no doubt, by bequests from some of the twelve prebendaries who had died in the interval[2]. There were duplicates and even triplicates, a natural result of the indiscriminate acceptance of bequests. Something more was required

---

[1] The Treasurer's Accounts for 1596 contain a charge of 30s. for 'scowringe the Armour.' A carpenter's bill (*Munim.* 40,813) has: 'worke done in the librare about the armor, begun the x daye of November and ended the xiiii day, 1601': it would seem from this that the armour followed the books, when they were moved out of the house over the east cloister some time between 1591 and 1597. Later references occur in the Treasurer's Accounts of 1603, when morrans, swords, muskets, &c. were bought for ci^s iiii^d, and also 100 lbs of gunpowder: and in those of 1605, 'paid to Rice Williams for watching and warding with munition and shott during the sicknes and funerall of our late Queene Eliz., and also for chardges at the coronation of our most gracious soveraigne King James—vi^li x^s.'

[2] As, for example, by the bequest of William Latymer, who died shortly before 15 Oct. 1583: for in a copy of Melanchthon, *Annotationes in Evangelia* (Frankfurt, 1544), we find: 'Gulielmus Latymerus, nuper unus prebendariorum huius ecclesiae, hunc librum dono dedit bibliothecae huius collegii Westmonasteriensis. 1584.' [H. 7. 5.]

than 'sweeping every other day.' Rearrangement and cataloguing called for another kind of caretaker than was contemplated in the Statutes. The services of the under-master, no less a genius than William Camden[1], were to be secured, and rewarded by the meagre stipend of a pound a year[2]. Under date of 16 May 1587 we read (f. 208):

1. It is decreed by the Deane and Chapter, whose names are underwritten, that the librarie of the Colledge shalbe furnished with shelves, deskes and all thinges necessarie thereunto.

2. Item that an Inventarie shalbe taken of all the bookes perteynyng therunto, and thre copies therof to be made, and thone to remaine in the librarie, the 2^d to be kept with Mr Deane, and the third to remaine with the Subdeane for the tyme being.

3. Item that all such bookes as be duble or triple shalbe sold or exchaunged, keping the best for the librarie, and the price or valew of the said bookes to be bestowed upon other bookes fytt for the same.

4. Item that Mr Deane, M^r d. Bonde, M^r d. Woode, Mr Grante, Mr Monford, and Mr Webstare, or any two of them with Mr Deane, shall sell, alter, change, and buy such necessarie bookes as be superfluous, or necessarie for the said librarie.

5. Item that Mr Deane, and everie prebendarie that will, shall have a key therof.

6. Item that Mr Camden, usher for the tyme present, or the usher or a peticannon herafter, by the apoyntment of Mr Deane, shall be keper of the said librarie, who shall have a care to kepe cleane, order, and dispose, and safelie preserve the same, and, for his paynes there imployd, shall have yearlie xx^s.

7. Item it is decreed, that a table shalbe kept of the names of all such benefactors, as either have or herafter shall bestow any bookes upon the said librarie.

We now come to the formal assignment to the Library of the room which it at present occupies. This was ordered on 3 Dec. 1591 (f. 223 *b*).

It is decreed by Mr Deane and Prebendaries whose names be underwritten, that the old dorter, and great rome before it, shalbe converted th'one to a librarie, thother to a schole for the Q. schollers, to be repaired and furnished to those good uses, upon contribution of such godlie disposed persons, as have and will contribute thereunto, and the same schole and librarie to be begun in the next spring, and the mony collected to the use therof, to be receaved by D. Grant, and th' accompte of the said receiptes to be made by him to Mr Deane and prebendaries present.

Edward Grant, one of the prebendaries whose names are signed

---

[1] Camden was undermaster from 1575 to 1593, and then headmaster till 1598. For two years at least he sang in the choir (*Treas. Acct.* 1584–5, 1585–6), he and William Heather being lay-clerks at the same time. For his gift of books in 1623 see below, p. 40.

[2] It is curious that in spite of this Order, and of the sentence in the Statute which was probably inserted about this time (*supr.* p. 13), the Treasurer's Accounts shew no fee for the Library-keeper until 1606 (*infr.* p. 17).

to this Order, was the schoolmaster. The money, however, for the school was slow in coming in: for we read on 7 May 1599:

It is decreed by Mr Deane and the Prebendaries present, that in respect that the now Scholehowse is to low and to litle to conteyne the number of Schollers, that the old Dorter, of late yeares begun to be made a larger Schole, shalbe, with all convenient spede, turned to that good use, for the benefytt of the Schollers, by such charitable contributions as may be gathered for the fynishing therof[1].

Although the Library had still to wait more than twenty years for its great benefactor, we may assume that the books were moved from the 'Prebends Lodginge' soon after the Order of 3 Dec. 1591 into the northern portion of the old Dorter. They had evidently been gone some time when the lease of 1606 was granted: doubtless they went before Thomas Griffith and Thomas Goodman entered into possession in 1597.

On 19 May 1606, in Dean Neile's first year of office, the following Order was made:

That from hense forth ther shalbe paid to Gabriell Birkhede 20^s per annum for the keepinge of the library, according to a former Chapter decree.

The reference seems to be to the original Order of 3 Dec. 1591. The Treasurer's Accounts shew that Gabriel Birkhead[2] was regularly paid from 1606 to his death in 1614. His successors were James Montaigne (1615), Robert Prichard (1618), Edward Hooper (1619), Richard Gouland (1620).

The following items from the Treasurer's Accounts of this period may find a place here.

1572. To Mr Carkett In Reward for Writing an old Cronycle of Westm^r, x^s.
1608. To Simon Paterson for bindinge the old written bible in folio which the Schollers reade in the Hall, iiii^s.
1613. For mendinge the library locke, xii^d.
1616. For mendinge the Close windows in the Library, xxxi^s.

The advent of Dean Williams, 10 July 1620, marks a new era in the

[1] In a bill of 1601-2 we find: 'the new scholehouse beinge ripped, and other the Prebends Lodgings therto adioyninge beinge ripped' [*Munim.* 40,982]. This was in the first year of Dean Andrewes.

[2] He was Dean Goodman's godson, and a Westminster scholar. He was buried in the cloisters, 23 Dec. 1614. He was probably grandson of Anne Birkhed who died in 1568, aged 102; and son of Christopher Birkhed who died in 1595, aged 77 (Chester, *Registers*). Christopher Birkhed was a lay-clerk (Treas. Accts), and Thomas Birkhead was a prebendary from 1551 to 1554. Gabriel, who was doubtless named after the Dean, held various offices: sacrist (1584), bell-ringer (1600). A copy of Cranmer's Bible in the Library [Zz 6 9] contains in the calendar at the beginning entries of the births and deaths of members of the Birkhed family.

R. W.   2

history of the Library. He at once introduced a true scholar, Richard Gouland, as Librarian, and soon procured him an increased stipend.

31 July 1622. It is further also decreed at this present Chapiter, that the Librarye Keeper shall have besides the olde allowance he hath allreadye of 20^s per annum, a new allowance of 8^{li} per annum more, to be accrewinge out of these two houses within the Colledge close, lately demised to John Packer Esquire, and Thomas Alisbury Esquire.

The Treasurer's Account for 1623 shews a payment

For writinge out the Catalogg of the bookes belonging to the Colledge Library, ii^s vi^d.

The smallness of this payment may afford some indication of the size of the Library before Williams with splendid liberality took it in hand. What he did may be told first in the florid language of his chaplain and biographer, Bishop Hacket[1]:

With the same generosity and strong propension of mind to enlarge the Boundaries of Learning, he converted a wast Room, situate in the East side of the Cloysters into *Plato's* Portico, into a goodly Libarary, model'd it into decent Shape, furnished it with Desks and Chains, accoutred it with all Vtensils, and stored it with a vast Number of Learned Volumes: For which use he lighted most fortunately upon the Study of that Learned Gentleman Mr *Baker* of *Highgate*, who in a long and industrious Life had Collected into his own possession the best Authors in all Sciences, in their best Editions, which being bought at 500l. (a cheap Peny worth for such precious War) were removed into this Store-House. When he received Thanks from all the professors of Learning in and about *London* far beyond his expectation, because they had free admittance to such Hony from the Flowers of such a Garden, as they wanted before, it compell'd him to unlock his Cabinet of Jewels, and bring forth his choicest Manuscripts. A Right Noble Gift in all the Books he gave to this *Serapæum*, but especially the Parchments. Some good Authors were confer'd by other Benefactors, but the richest Fruit was shaken from the Boughs of this one Tree, which will keep green in an unfading Memory in despite of the Tempest of iniquity. As *Pliny* the younger wrote in an Epistle upon the Death of his Son, *quatenus nobis denegatur diu vivere, relinquamus aliquid quo nos vixisse testemur*; so this Work will bear Witness to Posterity, that he liv'd, and that he liv'd beneficently. I borrow that assurance from honour'd Mr *Selden* in his Epistle before the History of *Eadmerus* Dedicated to the Founder of this Library, to whom he writes in these Words; *Egregius peritissimusque literarum censor, et fautor indulgentissimus et audis, et vere es. Quippe qui Doctrinam suo merito indies cupientissimus honestas: et sumptuosam in struendis publico usui Bibliothecis operam impendis. Praemium ita studiosis et armarium etiam sine exemplo solicitus parandi.* Yet what an ill requital did these unthankful times make him, when they removed that worthy Scholar, the Bibliothecary, whom he had placed, Mr *Richard Gouland*? whom he pick'd out above all men for that Office, being inferior to none in the knowledg of good Authors, Superiour to any for Fidelity and Diligence of so

[1] John Hacket and George Herbert went up to Trinity as Westminster scholars at the Election of 1608.

mortified a Life, that he could scandalize none but with Innocency and Piety ; nor offend any but by Meekness and Inoffensiveness. Such times, such Fruits[1].

Even the eulogy of his admirer cannot exaggerate the work which Williams did. The room itself, which was largely rebuilt by him, and its furniture are well described by Mr J. W. Clark (*loc. cit.*). The books which he gave, to the number of 2000, are entered in a handsome parchment volume, which shews how many of the public men of his day were laid under contribution by him[2]. And a full and formal recognition of his services on the part of the Chapter is preserved in the following Order of 27 Jan. 1626, soon after he had lost the royal favour and had been forced to surrender the Great Seal:

Whereas the Right Hon[ble] and Right reverend Father in God, John Bisshop of Lyncolne, one of his ma[ties] most Hon[ble] privye Councel, and Deane of the collegiate church of S[t] Peter in Westm[r], hath beene pleased to reedifye our college Library and the same to replenish with bookes to the vallue of Two thousand pounds at his owne propper costs and charges.

And whereas M[r] Richard Gouland M[r] of Artes hath taken very great and assiduous paines for thes two last yeares as in the choice so in the well ordering and disposition of the said bookes :

We therefore the Deane and chapiter of this Collegiate church for the perpetuall preservation of the said bookes to the good use thay were intended by the said Right reverend Father : as also in recompence of the paines of the said Richard Gouland, do with an unanimous Consent constitute and appoint him the said Richard Gouland Keeper of our said Colledg Lybrary, during the Tearme of his naturall life, the said Office to be executed by him self or his sufficient deputy, and do hereby give unto him during the said Tearme all that antient Stipend, or Fee of Twenty shillings, together with an increase of Nineteene pownds per annum, which said Summe is to be raised in forme following :......

Allso we further agree and consent that the said Richard Gouland shall have and enioy, a diet at the Deane and prebendaries table : together with all vailes, profitts, and Commodities to his place belonging.

Lastly at this present chapiter it is resolved and agreed that for his better Conveniency, and attendance uppon the said Office, he shall have and enioy in the nature of a dwelling house, that roome betwixt the Lybrary and the Schoole, which we do by this present assigne to him, or his deputy, or deputies, and to their Successors in that office for ever : allowing allso in his absence to his deputy, his commons with the officers of our colledg.

At the same Chapter was granted :

Richard Gowland a Patten of the office of the Keeper of the Colledg Library, fee per annum xx[ti].

We shall have to speak presently of the room between the Library and the schoolroom, which was thus assigned to the Librarian. We may now follow the fortunes of Mr Richard Gouland.

---

[1] Hacket's Life of Williams: *Scrinia Reserata*, 1693, i. 46 f.
[2] See below, pp. 39, 42, where the full list of his manuscripts is also given.

When Williams was deprived of the Great Seal, in October 1625, among his parting requests to the King was included a petition 'that his Majesty would please to bestow the next Prebend in Westminster that was void upon his Library-keeper, as his Father had promis'd.'[1] Nothing came of this, but in 1632 Williams gave him a prebendal stall at Lincoln.

On 11 Feb. 1650 it was agreed 'at a Meetinge of the Governors of the Schoole and Almeshouses of Westminster,'

Upon readinge of Mr Gowland's Petition and upon Consideration of his inability of body by reason of his weakness and sicklyness which Doth Disinable him to Attend the Service of Library Keeper of the Library belongeinge to the Schoole of Westm^r,

that Mr Gowland should receive £160 provided he should deliver up his Patent (*Munim.* 43,165).

And on 24 Sept. 1651 it was agreed 'to pay unto Mr Goland the Summe of Six pounds which he laid out for a Leidger Booke of Vellam' (*Munim.* 43,296). This doubtless refers to the great book in which the Benefactors of the Library are recorded.

He was buried in the north cloister, 15 Nov. 1659, 'after a painful and wearisom Pilgrimage in a weak and sickly body.' He left £10 to purchase for the Library 'the choicest pieces of the works of John Gerrardus, Vossius, and Salmatius' (Chester, *Registers*)[2].

In November 1650, after Mr Gouland had retired, we find carpenter's and plumber's bills, amounting to about £6, for repairing the roof of the Library. As the same accounts include an item 'for mending Coll. Humphreyes house broken downe with the stones,' it seems likely that a fall from the church had damaged both the Library and the adjoining house over the east cloister (*Munim.* 43,213 A—D).

The following documents carry on the story of the room between the Library and the schoolroom which had been assigned to Mr Gouland 'in the nature of a dwellinghouse.'

Munim. 43,292*.

In obedience to your Honours order July 12th 1651 I survey'd the roome ioyning to the Library which conteineth as followeth.

Imp. In Bredth 34 foote
In length 24 foote
All which conteineth 7 square of flowring
The charge will amount to 12^{li} 10 0.

---

[1] Hacket's Life of Williams, II. 25.

[2] The books actually purchased with his money are recorded in the great book of donors, f. 80b.

Three windowes to bee taken out of the Roofe of the said roome which conteining 12 lights apeece the charge of each window will bee 7^{+i} 0 0.

The Partition which goes crosse this roome will make good the Wall next the Schoole

The charge of this worke will amount to 33^{+i} 10 0.

These are returnd in obedience to your Honours Order.

Adam Browne.

Munim. 43,486 [Report of a Committee, 21 Nov. 1653].

Upon the Retorne of the Report of Mr Adam Browne, Surveyor, Concerning the Roome adioyning to the Library The Committee is of oppinion that the said Roome be made fitt and soe many Stalls made as will Receive the Manuscripts of Dr Williams, the Charge whereof will Amount to about 40^{+i} which the Committee thinke fitt to make Report to the Governors on Saturday next.

Munim. 43,487.

In obedience to your Honours order of the 10th of this present Decemb. 1653, Mr Busby and I have viewed that part of the Library, which is sett apart for the Manuscripts, and hee thinkes 6 foote from the partition will bee sufficient for that use.

The charge of the partition in timber worke will be 12 square at 25^s the square, that is in summe 15^{tt} : in playstering there will bee 200 yards, which will bee the charge of 9^{tt} : besides there must bee a window made into that roome, of which the charge 3^{tt}.

So the total charge will bee—27^{tt}.

[An estimate for a new Curtain for the Schoolroom follows, and the whole is signed by Adam Browne.]

The care thus bestowed was fatal to the collection of manuscripts; for they perished in a fire which broke out here at the end of 1694. (Widmore, *Hist.* pp. 164 f.)

II.

THE REMAINS OF THE MONASTIC LIBRARY OF WESTMINSTER ABBEY.

The following is an attempt at a list of books lost or extant which we know to have been in the Library of the Abbey at the time of the dissolution. It is only an attempt. I have not been able to make so careful a search for Westminster books as for those belonging to some other houses. Nevertheless, as will be seen, the survey has included a considerable number of libraries. One drawback about the Westminster books is that, so far as I can see, they are only identifiable by means of definite inscriptions contained in them. In other words, there was no such system of press-marks in use at the Abbey as prevailed at Canterbury, Ely, Bury, Norwich, and other places.

First, in the three bibliographical compilations of the fourteenth and fifteenth centuries, the *Liber Septem Custodiarum*, the *Registrum Angliae*, and Boston of Bury (all as yet unpublished, quoted by me from transcripts in my possession), the name of Westminster occurs as no. 11 in the list of libraries of which account is taken[1]. But in the texts of all three, so far as I have seen, there is but a single instance of this library being cited: it is adduced as containing a copy of Origen's Homilies on Joshua in the *Registrum Angliae*. In the *Liber Septem Custodiarum* a reference to another library takes its place, and in Boston both are absent. In a word, we gain nothing from these sources.

Next, I give a transcript of the notes taken by Leland in the library (*Collectanea* IV. 48, 49).

---

[1] The three compilations in question are all constructed on the same system. Their object was to show what books were to be found in the principal monastic and Cathedral libraries of England. A list of libraries was drawn up, each of which was denoted by a numeral. Then followed a list of writers with the titles of the works of each, and to each work was attached a group of numerals showing in what libraries it existed. The undertaking was initiated by the Franciscans, and expanded by Boston of Bury, but never completed.

In bibliotheca Petrina Westmonasterii.

1. Tabula Gulielmi Sudbiry, monachi Westmon : super Lyram.
2. Meditationes Roberti Grostest.
3. Sermones ejusdem.
4. Sermones Radulphi Eleemosynarii, Prioris de Hurteley (= Hurley), coenobioli prope Henleam super Tamesim, quod cella est monachorum Westmon. Leyland. Liber justum volumen est, inchoatum quidem motore Laurentio, abbate Westmon : sed absolutum illo mortuo, et Gualtero dedicatum, qui Laurentio successit. Repperi etiam in indice bibliothecae Westmon : hunc Radulphum postea abbatem fuisse Westmon : Sunt etiam in eadem bibliotheca Omeliae nomine Radulphi, abbatis Westmon : Sermonum vero liber sic incipit : *Ecce fratres dilectissimi.*
5. Tractatus Johannis Bromyard, applicans jura canonica et civilia ad materiam moralem.
6. Additiones Roberti G(r)ostest in libros Damasceni de ortodoxa fide, quos sciolus quidam male e Graeco transtulerat, id quod Robertus beneficio correcti exemplaris Graeci fecit.
7. Tabula Gul: Sudbury, monachi Westmon: super libros sancti Thomae de Aquino.
8. Prophetiae Joannis, canonici de Bridlington.
9. Tractatus Joannis Colton, archiepiscopi Armacani, pro sedatione scismatis.
10. Determinatio Thomae Palmer de ord: Praedicatorum in materia scismatis.
11. Determinatio Nicolai Fakenham de ordine Minorum.
12. Determinatio Akon Praed: de materia scismatis.
13. Determinatio Nicolai Rischton de scismate.
14. Armacani sermones 89, partim coram pontifice Ro(mano)ᴬᵛⁱⁿⁱᵒⁿⁱ, partim etiam in Anglia dicti. *Cum jejunas, unge caput.*
15. Armacani liber contra fratres mendicantes, continens in se 16 libellos.

It should be remembered that Leland's habit is to note the British authors whose works he found in libraries. The numbers are my own addition. We may be fairly confident that nos. 9—13 were in one volume.

Next comes Bale's *Index Scriptorum* (ed. Poole and Bateson). In this there are twelve references to books at Westminster. But of these, eleven (on pp. 13, 43, 214, 298, 348, 407, 408, 409, 419, 461, 488) all refer to one volume, probably written at Hexham, and now at Corpus Christi College, Cambridge (no. 139), which was in Bale's time at Westminster.

The remaining one (p. 165) is Henry of Huntingdon's History.

From John Joscelin's (Abp Parker's secretary) list of English historical writers preserved in Nero C. III. and printed by Hearne (*Robert of Avesbury*, p. 269), we learn that a Mr Pekyns[1], Prebendary of Westminster, owned either the volume just mentioned (C. C. C. 139)

---

[1] For Mr Pekyns, see above, p. 13.

or a transcript of it, or a sister-book,—anyhow, a book which contained several of the same items as C. C. C. 139.

The following is the very meagre list of extant Westminster manuscripts of the monastic library which I have been able to collect:

London. British Museum.
    Cotton. Claudius A. VIII. ff. 16—65. Richard Sporley's extracts from Flete, and a life of Abbot Esteney by John Felix.
        Otho C. XI. Abbot Ware's Consuetudinary.
        Titus A. VIII. A Chartulary (XIV.) including Sulcard and a letter of Osbert of Clare.
        Faustina A. III. A Chartulary (XIII. late) including Sulcard.
    Royal. 2. A. XXII. Westminster Psalter: see *Missale Westm.* (H. Bradshaw Soc.) III. p. xiv.
       ? 3. B. X. Gervase of Chichester. A transcript is in the Chapter Library. In both this volume and 13. A. XIII. the name of John Stephynson occurs.
       5. B. VIII. Jerome de viris illustribus etc. XII. Liber ecclesie S. Petri Westm.
       7. D. XXI. Innocent de contemptu mundi etc. XIV. "Constat Thome Champney monacho Westm."
       7. F. II. Lincolniensis de veneno etc. XIV.
       9. F. IV. Tabula Gul. Sudbury in libros S. Thomae Aquinatis. This is doubtless the copy seen by Leland (p. 23, no. 7). No pressmark surviyes; but, as Dr G. F. Warner (to whose kindness I owe my knowledge of this book) suggests, so portentous a work is hardly likely to have been copied. It occupied the compiler for sixteen years, from 1382: this volume contains 399 leaves.
       10. E. II. Gratian. Has a note at the end of an occurrence at Westminster in St Margaret's parish in the year 1300.
Lambeth.
    184. Egidius de regimine principum. XV. late. Has the arms of the Abbey: belonged to John Foxe (? the prebendary, 1606–23).
    761. Vita S. Edwardi. XIII.
        Lent by Abbot Islip to Abbot Seabroke of Gloucester.
Sion College.
    Arc. L. 40. Gospel of Nicodemus etc. in English verse, XIV.—XV. "Pertinet fratri Joh. holonde monacho Westm."
Oxford. *Bodleian Library.*
    MS. Bodley 46. Distinctiones Mauricii.
        Liber d. Th. Jay monachi Westm. ex dono eiusdem confratris egregii uiri d. Rob. humfrey cuius anime etc. (XV.)
        Ashmole 842. A Coronation book "*temp.* Ed. I. or earlier."
    Rawlinson C. 425. Pontificale Abbatiae Westmon: XIV.
    Rawlinson Liturg. g. 10. Litany, etc. XIV. late.
        (For these two see *Missale Westm.* III., vii., xii.)
    Colleges.
    Univ. 97. Gesta Romanorum. Hampole etc. XV.

Balliol. 264. Forma Religiosorum. xv.

"Starrys, monachi Westm : " (? *leg.* Stanys).

St John's. 147. Hampole : Lives of Saints. xv.

"Will. Grant et Will. Grove monachorum Westm." (? *leg.* Grene).

178. Neckam, Pseudo-Aristotle, Bestiary etc. xiii.

190. Bonaventura, sermons, etc., xiii. late, "ex procuratione fr. Will. de Hasele. Fuit domini Will. de Feltham, vicarii quondam de ...ayhe, cuius anime, etc."

Cambridge. *University Library.*

Ff. 1. 28. Ricardi de Cirencestria Speculum Historiale. xiv. The only known copy. "As the initials of the chapter relating to Westminster Abbey are specially elaborate, we may infer that this was the Abbey copy of the book." (J. E. B. Mayor, in Rolls Series edition, ii. clxv.)

Kk. 5. 29. Extenta maneriorum. Mostly xiv. early : containing the name of Thomas Jay.

Colleges.

Corpus Christi. 139. Simeon of Durham, etc. See above, p. 23.

197. Westminster continuator of Higden (see *Proc. of Brit. Acad.* vol. iii.).

Trinity. B. 10. 2. Apocalypse and pictures of the life of St Edward.

O. 7. 37. Medica. xi.—xii., xiii. "Ecclesie Petri Westm., per Tedyngton monachum." (xiii.)

Manchester.

Chetham Library. 6712. Flores Historiarum : containing the names of R. Teddington and T. Gardener.

Dublin. Trinity College.

B. 2. 7 (172). Lives of Saints. xiii. and xiv. "Ecclesie b. Petri Westm."

E. 2. 32 (548). Flete de fundatione Westm. xv. (fragment).

The Dean gives me the following note on the monks mentioned in the above list :

John Flete, writer of the history of Westminster Abbey and the lives of the abbots down to 1386. Entered the monastery 1420 : prior from 1456–65.

Richard Sporley extracted the main part of Flete's history *verbatim*, only inserting a short and untrustworthy account of the abbots before St Dunstan's time. Entered 1428.

John Felix sung his first mass in 1529.

Thomas Champney : first mass 1490.

John Holonde : first mass 1472, sub-prior in 1500 at Abbot Islip's election.

Thomas Jay : first mass 1509, prior 1528–35.

Robert Humfrey : first mass 1492, keeper of Lady Chapel in 1500.

John Stanys, keeper of Lady Chapel 1483, died 1485.

William Grant : first mass 1469, refectorar in 1500.

William Grene : first mass 1492, still living in 1525.

William de Hasele : mentioned in Bodl. Ashm. MS. 842, f. 86*b*, as attesting the miracle of the resuscitation of a boy drowned at Paddington *temp.* Hen. III. : compiler of the Westminster Customary, 1266.

R. Tedyngton : entered 1428.

Thomas Gardener : first mass 1501, still living in 1525.

III.

THE MANUSCRIPTS IN THE CHAPTER LIBRARY OF WESTMINSTER BETWEEN 1623 AND 1694.

Among the lost manuscript libraries of England that of Westminster Abbey has to be reckoned. I do not refer to the library possessed by the monks before the dissolution; the few surviving relics of that (as we have seen) are to be found in widely scattered collections, and probably not more than a single volume remains in its ancient home. The manuscripts with which I am here concerned are those given to the refounded library, mostly by John Williams (Dean of Westminster 1620—1641) on July 10th, 1623. Their life as a collection was a lamentably short one In November, 1694, they perished in a fire.

It is curious to note how scanty is the information which is pro-curable on the subject of this fire. Widmore in his *History* gives almost the only clear statement of the facts. His words are (p. 164):

" In the latter end of the year 1694, the manuscripts belonging to the library of this church were all burnt, except one. The occasion of the fire variously reported: there were in number about 230; all or most of them the gift of bishop Williams, the founder of the library. Several of these were of good value, and some of them no where else to be found; in that respect therefore it was a loss not to be repaired."

In the Chapter account books of the period there is an entry of expenditure incurred in repairs: but it is such as to throw no light on the exact date of the accident nor to define the extent of the mischief. It is probable that some news-letter or other journalistic source may be in existence which would be of assistance here, but so far I have been unable to lay hands upon it.

Details of the accident, however, interesting as they would be, are not essential to my present purpose. I desire in these pages to set out with as much clearness as possible the information which we possess as to the lost books themselves. In this respect we are better off than we might have anticipated.

Three separate catalogues of the manuscripts are in existence, one of them in print and another in more than one manuscript copy.

A.   The second in date, but probably the first in importance, is a catalogue made in 1672, perhaps for the purposes of the compilers of the

Oxford *Catalogi manuscriptorum Angliae et Hiberniae*, but ultimately not included in that work. It forms part of a rather large collection of catalogues, of which more than one copy exists in manuscript. The one which I have used as the basis of my text is at Trinity College, Cambridge (MS. O. 5. 38), another is Harley 694 (collated by me), and a third which I have also seen is at Oxford (MS. Tanner 272). In this the number of volumes described is a little over 180. I have taken this list as the standard of comparison with the other two.

B. The earliest is contained in the Register of the old library in possession of the Dean and Chapter of Westminster. This is a handsome seventeenth century vellum book containing entries of benefactions to the Library from the time of Williams (1623) to 1750. On ff. 122—129 of this volume is a list of the manuscripts, of which a careful transcript was most kindly made for me by the Rev. A. S. Duncan Jones. I have myself excerpted from the register such entries of manuscripts as occur mixed up among those of printed books in other parts of the volume. In the list of manuscripts proper there are something over 170 entries.

C. The third and last is the list compiled by Michael Maittaire for the *Catalogi manuscriptorum Angliae et Hiberniae*, and printed therein (Oxford, 1697, II. 1. 27). The descriptions in this are very brief. The number of items is 230.

Each of these three lists has certain entries peculiar to itself which will be duly set forth : but one fact has to be noted in this place.

At the end of bishop Williams's gifts in the Register (B) there is an account of certain books, four in number, given by Sir Robert Cotton. The contents of these are enumerated at considerable length. In the Trinity College list (A) the same books are elaborately catalogued, but nothing is said about their donor. Other volumes of similar character occur in company with them. None of these are certainly recognizable in Maittaire's list (C). Now, a passage in Wharton's *Anglia Sacra* (II. 345), coupled with Smith's Catalogue of the Cottonian MSS., makes it quite clear that the books in question, whether given or lent by Sir Robert Cotton to Westminster, were eventually returned to the Cottonian Library and were there marked Otho C. XII., XIII., XIV., XV., XVI., Otho D. X., XI. All of them were either destroyed or damaged in the deplorable fire of 1731.

I print the three lists separately, and also a table showing which items are common to A, B, and C, and which are peculiar to each. A preserves a record of the distribution of the books in their cases.

Nos. 1—20 (in the combined list) were in Pluteus 10: 21—39 in Plut. 11: 40—65 in Plut. 12: 66—92 in Plut. 21: 93—113 in Plut. 22: 114—131 in Plut. 23: 132—148 in Plut. 24: 149—158 in Classis 25: 159—168 in Cl. 26: 169—182 in Cl. 27.

The number of volumes in each class is very small—20, 19, 26, 27, 21, 18, 17, 10, 10, 14—hardly more than could be accommodated on the shelves of a single large book-case. The manuscripts were kept in "stalls" (see p. 21) in a room at the end of the Library nearest to the school, i.e. the southern end; and the fire in which they perished was confined to that portion of the building.

The arrangement in A shows that a classification of the books according to subject was aimed at. Nos. 1—15 are Greek books, 16—20 are Latin grammarians, 21—65 Latin authors, Latin versions of Greek authors, and Humanists, 66—92 Bibles, Liturgical books, glosses, 93—131 Patristic and later Theological writers, 132—150 principally Theology, with some Civil and Canon Law, 151—163 principally Medicine, 164 Alchemy, 165—168 Astrology and Astronomy, 169—182 principally English History.

It is unsafe attempting to speculate on the age and general character and value of the books. The greater part of the classical MSS. were probably Italian copies of the fifteenth century: but a Seneca (no. 25) and a Virgil (no. 29) are described as ancient. Of the Theological collection we may call attention to no. 68 Psalterium perantiquuum, 93 Prosper etc., vetus exemplar, 123 containing Poems of St Boniface, 145 Oswaldi Regis Vita, 146 containing a *cantus comicus* of Thomas Claxton, 155 a Dioscorides in Latin with pictures, 103—105 Hebrew Bibles, 227 "Liber S. Edmundi Regis," 228 "a great folio of old English Poems," 229 "another, lesser." The volume described in list C, no. 129, as Expositiones SS. Patrum in Biblia, viz. Dionysii Ignatii Polycarpi Justini etc., *may* have been valuable and interesting, but I incline to suspect that it was a rather recent compilation.

List of Manuscripts formerly in the Chapter Library.

The continuous numbering in lists A and B is my own. The items which are peculiar to each list are marked with an asterisk.

A

With variants from MS. Harley 694 f. 20 (38) sqq. (= H). These are placed in square brackets.

Catalogus codicum manuscriptorum in Bibliotheca Westmonasteriensi anno 1672.

Pluteus 10.

1.	1.	Comment. in Epistolas Pauli. Graece.
2.	2.	Disputatio Georgii [Gregorii] Coressii contra Cornelium Praelectorem Pisanum. Graece.
3.	3.	Martyrologium. Gr.
4.	4.	Codini parecbolae [parabolae] Historicae de Byzantio. Gr.
5.	5.	Galenus περὶ κρίσεων. Gr.
6.	6.	Menologium. Gr.
7.	7.	Ap(h)thonii progymnasmata cum scholiis, et Hermogenes. Gr.
8.	8.	Ammonius, Michael Patricius, Alexander Aphrodis. et alii in Logicam Aristotelis. Gr.
9.	9.	Joannes Grammaticus de anima. Gr.
10.	10.	Anastasius de Hexaëmero. Gr. [+ etc. H.]
11.	11.	Platonis Definitiones [Distinctiones] etc. Gr.
12.	12.	Eman. Moschopuli Grammatica. Gr.
13.	13.	Aristotelis Organon. Gr.
14.	14.	Eman. Moschopuli Grammatica. Gr.
15.	15.	Pindari Olympia. Gr.
16.	16.	Prisciani Grammatica.
17.	17.	Prisciani Grammatica.
18.	18.	Nonius Marcellus.
19.	19.	Festus Pompeius.
20.	20.	Festus.

Pluteus 11.

21.	1.	Livius.
22.	2.	Livii pars altera.
23.	3.	Pars tertia Livii.
24.	4.	Donatus in Terentium.
25.	5.	Senecae Tragoediae.
26.	6.	Senecae Tragoediae.
27.	7.	Horatius de arte sua et Epistolae. [*om.* sua H.]
28.	8.	Virgilii Eclogae et Georgica.
29.	9.	Virgilii omnia.
30.	10.	Comment. vetus in Horatium. an Acronis ?
31.	11.	Horatii opera.
32.	12.	Juvenalis. Epistolae Plinii.
33.	13.	Orationes excerptae e Livio, etc.

34.	*14.	Discursus Italicus.
35.	15.	Ovidii Epistolae.
		Cicero de essentia mundi seu Timaeus.
36.	16.	Salustii omnia cum notis.
37.	17.	Lucanus.
38.	*18.	Virgilius.
39.	*19.	Radices Hebraicae.

Pluteus 12.

40.	1.	Sidonius Apollinaris.
41.	2.	Phaedo Platonis. Lat.
42.	3.	Plinii Epistolae charta.
43.	4.	Justinus.
44.	5.	Agellius charta. [5. A : gellius.]
45.	(6.	None.) [6. A. gellius chartâ.]
46.	7.	S. Hyeronomus de uiris illustribus.
		Aemilius Probus et Plinius de uiris illustribus
47.	8.	Xenophontis Ciropaedia. Lat.
48.	9.	Plinius Secundus de uiris illustribus.
49.	10.	Diodorus Siculus per Poggium. [+Lat. H.]
50.	11.	Valerius Maximus.
51.	12.	Asinus Luciani Latine per Poggium.
52.	13.	Cicero de officiis.
53.	*14.	Caesaris Malvicini poemata.
54.	15.	Eclogae Virgilii.
		Salustius.
55.	16.	Salustius.
56.	17.	Esopi Fabulae. De Lapidibus.
57.	18.	Lucanus.
58.	19.	ffabula Philodoxes. [-os H.]
59.	20.	Tibullus.
60.	21.	Petri Apollonii Poemata. [Apollinii H.]
61.	22.	De re oeconomica.
62.	23.	Tibullus.
63.	*24.	Tibullus.
64.	25.	Epistolae Nogarolae ad Ovannum etc. [Quannum H.]
65.	26.	Ovidius de arte.

Pluteus 21.

66.	1.	An English New Testament wᵗʰ a Calendʳ of yᵉ Epistles & Ghosples.
67.	*2.	Biblia Hyeronymi minore charactere.
68.	3.	Psalterium Latinum perantiquum. NB.
69.	4.	Alterum Psalterium forma minori.
70.	5.	Testamentum Latinum et Historia Evangelica.
71.	6.	An English New Testament.
72, 73.	7 (8).	A French New Testament in 2 Vol. Liber elegans.
74.	9.	An old Missal wᵗʰ yᵉ Roman Calendar before itt.
75.	10.	Another Missal.
76.	11.	Another Missal.
77.	12.	An old Latin Prayer Booke. in yᵉ end some Dutch.
78.	13.	Another English prayer booke.

79. 14. A Treatise how to live godlily begineth a Treatise y^t sufficeth to each man and woman to live after if they will be [wolen bee H.] saved.
80. 15. A book of prayers to certain Saints wth their [the H.] Pictures. Lat.
81. 16. Meditationes et orationes valde utiles. Liber imperfectus.
82. 17. Officium B. V. secundum consuetudinem Romanam : ibidem Psalmi 7 poenitentiales.
83. *18. Psalterium Latinum forma minuta.
84. 19. Liber exorcizandi[1] ritum continens initium sic[2]. Ordo ad faciendum[3] aquam etc.   [1] [exercitandi H.]   [2] [incipit H.]   [3] [-am H.]
85. 20. Glossae in omnes fere partes Bibliorum 20 libris contentae.
86. 21. Notationes in omnes Pauli Epistolas una cum Prologo. [Prologos etc. H.] Hyeronomi.
87. 22. Hyeronomi Biblia forma maxima.
88. 23. Hyeronomi Biblia forma minori.
89. 24. The Summary of ye whole Bible.   Collected by Wycliffe.
90. 25. Wiclifs (Bible) in English, 2 vol.   [Wyckliffe in Engl. H.]
91. 26.   „   „   „
92. 27. Epistolae Pauli cum Commento.

[*Pluteus*] 22.

93. 1. Prosper de vita contemplativa.   Cipriani Epistolae de opera et eleemosyna. [+Aug. de utilitate agendae Poenitentiae H.] Hugo Abbas Bruxellensis (1. Barzellensis) de Cohortatione Fratrum. [Patrum H.] S. Augustini sermo de laude et utilitate Spiritualium Canticorum.
94. 2. Chrisostomi homiliae. Lat.
95. 3. Hieronymi *Epistola de locis misticis.*   [Epistolae H.]
Idem contra Jovinianum.
Augustinus contra 5 Haereses.
96. 4. Ambrosius de Officiis.
97. 5. Augustini Sermones varii.
98. 6. Augustinus de Civitate dei.
99. 7. Richardus de S. Victore de Benjamin et Fratribus.
Augustinus de gratia Novi Testamenti.
100. 8. Varii Tractatus S. Augustini et Abbatis Cheremonis.
101. 9. Augustini Confessiones.
102. 10. Augustinus de Charitate
de vita et moribus Clericorum
item sermones duo.
103. 11. Augustinus de doctrina Christiana et
Sententiae Hugonis Parisiensis.
104. *12. Augustinus in Symbolum.
105. 13. Idem de animae quantitate.
Eiusdem Retractationes.
106. 14. Gregorii Moralia.
107. 15. Gregorii Nazianzeni orationes quaedam interprete Ruffino.
108. 16. Bedae Expositio in Epistolas Jacobi. Petri. Johannis. Judae.
109. 17. Gregorii Homiliae in Ezechielem.
110. 18. Isidorus Hispalensis comm. in Pentateuchum Josuam Judices et Regum.

Augustinus de animae quantitate et
de Retractationibus.
Hyeronimus in Acta Apostolorum.

111. 19. Isidorus in Pentateuchum iterum cum aliis nonnullis.
112. 20. Incerti de misterio Trinitatis et formatione creaturarum.
113. 21. Liber Summarum.

[*Pluteus*] 23.

114. 1. Josephi Historia. Lat. 2 vol. magna forma.
115. 2. Alexander Necham de naturis rerum.
116. 3. Ecclesiastes et Psalmorum liber.
117. 4. Varii tractatus Hugonis Parisiensis.
118. 5. Magister Sententiarum. Libri 4.
119. 6. Baldwinus de Sacramento Altaris.
120. 7. Baldwini Tractatus de commendatione fidei et alia.
121. 8. Liber Scintillarum.
122. 9. Homiliae quedam forte Ludovici de Granado Hisp.
123. 10. Alcuinus Presbyter de virtutibus [virtute H.] et vitiis cum nonnullis
aliis Basilii, Ambrosii, et Bonifacii.
Vita Eufrasiae et
Passio Julianae V.
124. 11. Gulielmus de Pagula de oculo dextro et sinistro sacerdotis.
125. 12. Versibus Anglicanis scriptus Liber forte Necham.
126. 13. Lincolniensis dicta comodifera Theologis et Praedicatoribus.
127. 14. A diologue, a Preacher and a Roman Priest written by some modern
author.
128. 15. Trattato di Missere Giovanni Dominico chiamato si doctrinale.
Cui additur la passione di dieci milia Crucifixi di Jesu Christi versa in
Italiano per Anastasio Gardiano de libri della sedia Apostolica.
129. 16. Lucerna conscientiae anonymi.
Innocentius de miseria conditionis humanae.
130. 17. An Exposition upon ye Commandm^ts and several treatises in old
English.
131. 18. Valerius Maximus.
Palladius de agricultura.
Augustinus de natura boni.
De Architectura.
De opere monachorum.

[*Pluteus*] 24.

132. 1. Codex Juris cum glossis praenotatur n [N^o H.] 20 deest 19.
133. 2. Expositiones in SS. Biblia Collecta ex antiquis Patribus Graecis et
Latinis. Liber continens Lyturgiam,
Postillas super Cantica
Sermones abbreuiatos Gorhami
Summam Grostestae et alia multa.
134. 3. Augustini, Hieronymi, Bedae, Hugonis, Ambrosii, Athanasii, Chrysostomi etc. opuscula.
135. 4. Ivonis Carnotensis Epistolae.
136. 5. Ivonis Carnotensis Epistolae.
Origenes super Leviticum.

		Psalterium B. Mariae.
137.	6.	Regula S. Benedicti.
		Martyrologium Romanum.
		Evangelia et Epistolae.
138.	7.	An English Poet de miseria Humanae vitae etc.
		A short Exposition upon yᵉ Lords Prayer etc. prose.
139.	8.	Othonis, Octoboni, aliorumque Constitutiones [aliorum consultationes H.].
140.	9.	Expositio Vocabulorum Biblicorum.
		Dictionarium Lat. et Angl.
141.	10.	Summa Magistri Thomae.
		Expositio in Psalmos.
142.	11.	Capitula Evangelii versu. [Evangeliorum H.]
		Summa de Casibus.
		Catalogus Episcoporum Romanorum notans tempus sessionis.
143.	12.	An Exposition upon yᵉ Decalogue. English.
144.	13.	Instructio Praelatorum in arte medicinae spiritualis.
145.	14.	Oswaldi Regis Vita.
146.	15.	Compendium Vitae spiritualis.
		Modus Confitendi.
		Speculum S. Edmundi.
		Tractatus Thomae Claxton.
147.	16.	Apparatus D. Portuodosimi [Pretnodosini H.] de processu Judiciario.
148.	17.	Piorum et Picorum genaeologiae [Genealogiae H.] per Jenettum [Jerrettum H.].

[*Pluteus*] 25.

149.	1.	Almansor. Lat.
150.	2.	Johannis Chrysostomi opuscula.
		Fulberti quaedam.
		Chrysostomi quaedam alia.
		Ambrosii quaedam.
		Hugonis Archidiaconi Epistolae [Epistola] ad Fulbertum.
151.	3.	Liber aureus de Medicina.
		Alfani Archiepiscopi liber de medicina.
		Herbarium s. synonymia herbarum.
		Alia quaedam medica.
		Tractatus de urinis.
152.	*4.	Liber Passionarium dictus.
153.	5.	Joannicius ad tegnum galeni.
		Viaticum.
154.	6.	Galfridus de Monmouth de gestis Britonum. Editus est sub nomine Turpini.
155.	7.	Dioscorides lat. cum ffiguris Plantarum pulchre pictis.
156.	7ᵃ.	Joannes a [de H.] S. Amando super Antidotarium Nicholai.
		Compendium Johannis Mesue.
		Prognosticatio Hippocratis.
		Abbreviatio Tabulae [Tabula H.] in Antidotarium.
157.	8.	Isaac de dietis.
		Glossae super tegnum Galeni.

158.   *9.   Gellii quaedam ut (vi)detur.   liber principio et fine mutilus.
Comment. in Evangelia et Epistolas.

Cl(assis) 26.

159.   1.   Avicenna.
160.   2.   De re medica scriptores varii.
161.   3.   Medicinae liber.
162.   4.   Bernardi Medicinale.
163.   5.   Bernardus de Gordonio de regimine Morborum.
164.   6.   Tractatus varii de Chymica.
165.   7.   Julii Materni Firmici Matheseos libri charta scripti.
166.   8.   Joh. Sacrobosco computus.
Algorismus et alia.
167.   9.   Galenus de febribus.
168.   10.   Sphaera Apuleii.   [H. omits the number 10.]
Liber Astrologicus.
Opus Philosophorum.
Astrologicum opusculum.
Liber Revolutionum Lunae
Bernardi de Gordonio opuscula.
Guidonis Astronomia.   [Anatomia H.]
Arnoldi Phlebotomia et alia.
Gerardi quaedam.

[Pluteus] 27.

169.   1.   Historia Brittonum.   English.
170.   2.   Chronicon S. Albani. incipit. *Britannia quae nunc dicitur Anglia.*
Chronicon imperatorum Romanorum.
171.   3.   Benedictus Abbas de gestis Henrici secundi.
172.   4.   Gyraldus Cambrensis descriptio Walliae.
173.   5.   Roberti Lincoln. monitoria Epistola ad priorem de Newham etc.
(=Otho C. xv.)

Regula S. Augustini de vita clericorum et alia.
Consuetudinarium sive rituale.
Fragmentum homiliae Saxonicae.
Ordo Conuertorum (*sic*).
Gulielmus de Mandagoto de electionibus faciendis.
(27)   Lincoln. de 7 Sacrimentis (!).
Idem de forma Confitendi.
Inventio musicae per sonum Malleorum.
De periculis quae accidunt circa officium sacerdotis.
174.   *6.   Historia Britaniae.   (=Otho C. xiii.)
175.   7.   Calendarium rerum Anglicarum.   (=Otho C. xvi.)
Chronicon Rogeri Cestrensis.
Vita R. Grosthead per Richardum [Nich: H.] monachum.
Martirium S. Hugonis Lincoln.
Roger Dimocke contra Lollardos.
Passio S. Kenelmi Regis.
De S. Edwardo Rege.
De S. Guthlaco martyre.
Vita S. Elphegi Archiepiscopi.

Vita S. Johannis Beverlacensis.

Historia Joh. Beverlac. per Folchardum monachum.

A Sermon in defence of yᵉ Scripture in English.

Constitutiones Ecclesiae Eboracensis.

176.   8.   Passionarium.
177.   9.   Decreta Ecclesiastica H. Spelman.
178. 10.   Historia quaedam de Regno Angliae in quo varii tractatus Historici.
                                                                    (=Otho D. xi.)
179. *11. Varii tractatus inter quos quaedam Roberti Grosthead.
180. *12. Varii tractatus Grosthead.   (=Otho C. xiv.)
            Regum, Paparum, et Cardinalium Epistolae.
            De Formoso papa. in hoc vol. alia multa continentur v. in. p. adversa
            A. 12. B. 4.
181. 13.   Grosthead opera.   (=Otho D. x.)

[Here follows in H. Codex 1ᵐᵘˢ. Elenchus Contentorum in hoc Codice.
It is no. 173 in this list.]

182. *1.   Articles del Waldmote [Wardmote H.] in London.
       2.   Ordinatio pro auxilio et contributione pro bonis mari ejectis.
       3.   Stat. 27. E. 1.   ⎧ Ordinatio de finibus.
                              ⎪ De onere vicecomitis.
                              ⎨ De rote. [retʳ H.]
                              ⎪ De nominibus repleg.   [hominibus H.]
                              ⎪ De gaolis deliberandis.
                              ⎩ Ordinatio Justic. de nisi prius.
       4.   Ordinatio de moneta apud Stebenhithe.
       5.   Ordinatio Civitatis London de placitis [et placitis H.] ibidem.
       6.   Compositio inter cives London. et Winton.
       7.   Les rules de Husbandry de Grosthead.
       8.   De ponderibus.
       9.   Les usages de Gavelkinde.
      10.   Ordinances pur le guarde de Londres.
      11.   De tenentibus in civitate de London.
      12.   De damnis prisonae. Penae coriptione temporis. [, Prisona, Poenae
            scriptione, tempore H.]
            Penae diversae ad festum Regis.
            Notae diuerse Irreplegiabiles per commune Brevae.   [breve H.]
            Repleg. [-iabiles H.] per Commune Breve.
      13.   Ordo tenendus a Civ. London. cum placita Coronae tenetur [tenentur
            H.] ad turrem London.
      14.   Assiza [-ae H.] Panis in London.
      15.   Assize in London. pro muris et stillicidiis.
      16.   Partitio Brevium in Orig. et Judic. et subdivisiones.
      17.   Magna Charta.
      18.   Charta de foresta.
      19.   De Merton.
      20.   Marleburge.
      21.   Westminster.   ⎫
      22.   Expositio vocabulorum. ⎭ [21 H.]
      23.   Statutum de Mercatoribus.

24. Statutum de Glocester et quo warranto.
25. Westminster 2.   [Will. 2. H.]
26. Nomina Regum Angliae Christianorum.
27. Breve super statutum de Winton.
28. De Westminster.
29. Statutum [-a H.] Scaccarii.
30. Distinctiones Scaccarii.   [H. adds 30.   Articuli de Moneta.
                              31.   De homag., fidelitate, et Ho-
                                   magio.
                              34.   Mortmaine.]
(31. Nothing.)
32. Articuli de Moneta.
33. De homag. foedalitate et homagio.
34. Mortmaine.
35. Sententia Excommunicationis lata super Magna Charta et Charta de
    ffloresta. [magnam Chartam et Chartam H.]
36. Dies Communes in [de H.] banco.
37. Extenta manerii [-orum H.]
38. Dictum de Kenelworth.
39. Exceptiones ad Brevia et ordo eorundem.
40. De Warranto.   [om. H.]
41. [40 H. which has no 41.] Summa que dicitur Fleta secundum Rad.
    de Hengham.
42. Modus ordinandi brevia in suis [s' H.] casibus.
43. Proprietas narrationum.
44. Summa Southampton.
45. Modus Calumniandi issonium.   [essonium H.]
46. Judicium Issoniorum.   [essen- H.]
47. Rageman.
48. Statutum de Millitibus.
49. Articuli Cōnon.   [om. H.]
50. Assiza Panis et Cervisiae.
51. Rageman ad inquirendi (!) contra [inquirend. coram H.] Justic.
    itinerantibus.
52. Statutum de quinto decimo.   [-a H.]
53. Regulae [Registrum H.] Cancellariae.   (= Otho D. xɪ.)

[The following are detailed descriptions of volumes already entered.]

178. 1. Historia quaedam de Regno Angliae et Regobus [-ibus H.] de Paschae
    observatione in Anglia et de primis Regalibus ornamentis regni
    Angliae.
    2. Genealogia D. Petri de Luxemburg comitis S. Pauli.
    3. Item Genealogia Duce [Dnᵃᵉ H.] Margaretae uxoris eius.
    4. L Office de Seneschall, de Bayliffe, de Provost, de Hayward, de Carvers
    [Carucis H.], de Chantres [Charetre H.], de Vacher, de Porcher, de
    Boucher [Bercher H.], de la daye de Seigneur des Accomptons
    [-lice H.] Galliere [Gallice H.]
    5. Tractatus de (re) Rustica s. [sive] oeconomica Gallier [Gallice H.]

6. Item de eadem materia s. [sive] de cura rei familiaris ad Comitissam Lincolniae [Nicholae H.] per Rob. Grostheade Ep. Lincoln. in eadem veteri Gallicana.

7. Institutio parandi cibos s. de [+arte H.] culinaria veteri in qua elucidantur vocabula ferculorum quae habentur in prandiis coronationum et installationum Gallice.

8. Liber de herbis salutaribus et gemmis pretiosis Gallice.

9. Decimae triennales. Antiqua Laxatio (Taxatio) beneficiorum appropriatio [-torum H.] et nova [-ae H.] cum [+feodis H.] militum et reditibus [redd- H.] et donationibus spectantibus ad quaedam monasteria in comitatu Eboracensi.

10. [11.] Prophetia [-icae H.] quaedam de iis que contingerent ad annum domini 1290 inter Germanos Italos Anglos Wallos et Scotos.

11. [10.] Littera Edwardi 3 Reg. Angl. universis declarantibus (!) [-tes H.] injurias sibi illatas a Philippo Valesio Reg. Franc.

12. Litera Benedicti Papae ad Edw. R. Angl. de causa inter papatum et Ludovicum Imperatorem.

13. Eiusdem litera ad eundem de componenda pace in(ter) Reges. Edw. et Philippum.

14. Edwardi quaedam litera ad Collegium Cardinalium et universarum caeli [ecclesiarum H.] praelatos de eadem materia.

15. De eadem controversia literas (?) [-ae H.] patentes ad uniuersos Reges [Rˢ H.] Johannis Bohemiorum aliorumque ducum et comitum.

16. Multae [Mutus H.] literae Ludovici [-ae H.] Imp. Rom. et [Ed. H.] Regis Angl. de eadem re.

17. Litera Ambaldi et Ramundi [Ray- H.] Cardinalium ad R. Edw. quod gaudent [-eat H.] et gaudere debeat de electione Clementis 6ᵗⁱ in papam, qui natus fuerit [-at H.] in ejus ducatu eique aliquando fidelitatis juramentum fecerit [-at H.] et de componenda inter priores (so) Reges pacem.

18. Litera R. Edw. ad Clerum Eboracensem ut faciant orationes et processiones pro se et exercitu proficiscente contra Gallos et Scotas.

19. Litera Nicholai Laurentii severi et Clementis Libertatis pacis justiciaeque tribuni et sacrae Romanae Reip. Liberatoris.

20. Litera R. Edw. ad Bartholomeum de Burgher(sh) Constabularium cartis [castri] Dovoriae et custodem 5 portuum de inhibendis provisionibus papalibus.

21. Eiusdem [+literae H.] ad omnes Episcopos Abbates Priores decanos officiarios [+etc. H.] et ad Vicecomitem Eboracensem super eadem materia.

22. Litera Regis [-iae H.] ad H. Ep. Lincoln. compatientes paupertati domus B. Mariae Ebor. et prohibentes collectores suos exigere medietatem tanam [Lanarum H.] aliasque decimas ab eadem quae ipsi ex decreto Parliamenti erant solvendae.

23. Tractatus de Articulis [+Justiciariorum H.] Itinerantium.

(=Otho C. xiv.)

173.   1. Roberti Ep. Lincolne monitoria Ep. ad priorem et conventum de Newham.

2. Visitatio eiusdem domus per Archidiaconum Lincoln. authoritate [+Dⁿⁱ H.] Papae anno 1232.

3. Consultatio de cohibendis Tartarorum incursionibus per processus, jejunia, orationes dominicas cum salutationibus etc.
4. Regula S. Augustini de vita Clericorum.
5. Constitutio vel potius ordinatio Canonicorum Regularium secundum Canonicam Regulam S. Augustini a Patribus instituta.
6. Consuetudinarium sive Rituale.
7. Fragmentum Homiliae Saxonicae.
8. Ordo conversorum.
9. Libellus a Mag. Will. de Mandagoto Archidiacono Nemausensi compositus super electionibus faciendis [+et earum processibus ordinandis H.].
10. Tractatus de 7 Sacramentis et comm. Casibus authore ut videtur Roberto Lincoln.
11. Modus sive forma confitendi secundum bonae memoriae Robertum Lincoln. Ep.
12. De Inventione Musicae per sonum malleorum super incudem.
13. Tractatus de periculis quae accidunt circa officium sacerdotis.

180.   Contenta in 20 [2do H.] Codice.   (=Otho C. XIV.)

*1. Epistolae Roberti Grosthead Ep. Lincoln.
2. Sermo Roberti quidem (!) [ejusdem H.] propositus coram papa et cardinalibus in Concilio Lugdunensi cum quadam Epistola.
3. Expositio brevis orationis dominicae.
4. Nomina Philosophorum.
5. Capitula Turstini Archiep. Ebor. ad Will. Cantuar. de reformatione et discordiis monachorum ecclesiae S. Mariae Ebor. A.D. 1132.
6. Epistolae quaedam Rhetoricae et Satyricae contra Malgerium et Rixvaldum [Rixvaldium H.].
7. Invectiva in quendam pro defensione [detentione H.] clarissimi viri R. Hereford. Episcopi.
8. Epistola quedam [quaerula H.] Abbatis Clarevallensis ad Lucium Papam super electione cujusdam ad Archiep. Ebor.
9. Idem ad Eugenium Papam super eadem re.
10. Ejusdem Epistola ad Cardinales Romanae [+Curiae H.] super predicti Willelmi electione.
11. Epistola Bernardi Abbatis ad Eugenium Papam pro Archiepiscopo Cantuar. contra Eboracensem et Winton super veteri quendam (!) [querea H.] de Rogatione.
12. Epistola Imarii [Ymari H.] Tusculani Ep. Carmone ei [+Canonicis H.] Ecclesiae London. super electione Richardi Ep.
13. Epistola Eugenii Papae Decano et Canonicis S. Petri in Episcopatu [et Epist. H.] Dunelmensi et Carleolensi super electione predicti Willelmi in Archiep. Ebor.
14. Epistola Abbatis Clarevallensis ad Innocentum Papam de erroribus Mag. Petri Abaelardi contra Calumnias objectorum capitulorum.
15. Eiusdem Epistola de eodem [eadem] ad Cardinales.
16. Responsio M. Petri Abaelardi contra Calumnias objectorum capitulorum.
17. Figuratae quaedam controversiae.
18. Epistola Henrici Imp. ad Philippum Reg. Galliae contra Papa(m) lectu dignissima.

19. Epistola Rhetorica ad monachum fugativum [fugit- H.].
20. Epistola Hugonis ad Epp. Dunelmens. et Carleolens. et canonicos Ebor. de electione predicti Willelmi.
21. Epistola Eugenii Stephano Regi Angliae de honora. de Richard. Ep. Lond. [de honorando Richardo Ep°. H.].
22. Epistola eiusdem ad Mathildam Reginam Angliae super eadem re.
23. Epistola Cardinalis Ep^i Hostiensis ad Canonicos London. super eadem re.
24. Epistola Alexandri Papae ad Theobaldum Archiep. Cant. in qua enarrat Historiam schismatis inter se et Octavianum.
25. Epistola Patriarcharum schismaticorum super electione et consecratione Octaviani.
26. Epistola cujusdam missa occultato nomine ad Papam Alexandrum.
27. Epistola Frederici Imp. Rom. de electione et consecratione sui Apostolici missa cunctis fidelibus ad confirmationem Electionis ejusdem.
28. Altercatio super Formoso papa.
   [Here follows in H.: Bibl. Westmonast. N. 12. B. 4.
   1 Articles de Wardmote etc. = no. 182 (Otho C. xii.)]

B.

THE LIBRARY REGISTER AT WESTMINSTER.

A folio volume of vellum recently rebound.

TITLE.

> *A Register or Catalogue of the Names of y^e Benefactours to the Publicque Librarie att Westminster.*

Anno Domini 1623.

f. 2. Dr John Williams Late ArchBp of Yorke formerly Lord Keeper of the Greate Seale of England and Deane of Westminster after that he had at his greate cost and charges repaired and fitted this Library as now it is gave the 10th of July An° Dn̄i 1623 towards the furnishing of it these Bookes following.

ff. 2—17^a. Double columns of about 32 lines each.   f. 17^b blank[1].

f. 18. Sr Julius Caesar.   20 Oct. 1623.   £128 (given and collected) spent on the books following.

20. The Cursitors of Chancery. 20 Oct. 1623.   £41. 12.
24. Sr Rich. Luson.   10 Jan. 1623.   £50.
25. Sr Toby Matthew.   24 Sept. 1624.   £50.
26. Francis Lo. Russell afterwardes Earle of Bedford. 8 May 1624. £10.
27. Sr Fran. Leigh.   20 June 1624.   £10.
28. Sr Randolph Crue.   4 July   „   £6. 13. 4.

---

[1] I do not, as a rule, give the titles of the *printed* books which are entered under the names of donors: but all entries of manuscripts.

f. 29. Sʳ Hen. Spilman. 22 Sept. 1624 £6. 13. 4.
30. Jo. Packer. 10 Oct. „ £10.
31. Sʳ Th. Canon. 6 Nov. „ £10.
32. Rob. Newell D.D. (preb.). 14 Dec. „ £6. 13. 4.
33. G. Darell D.D. (preb.). 25 Dec. „ £10.
35. Edw. Palmer (Fellow of Trinity). 13 May 1624. £20.
36. Jo. Seward. 18 Dec. 1624. £20.
37. Jo. Holt D.D. (preb.). 23 Dec. „ £20.
38. Rich. Oakeley. 28 Dec. „ £20 (spent on chains).
39. Jo. Sᵗ Alman. a pair of Globes, which cost him £27.
40. The Serieants of Law made of the call in 1623. £100.
42. Wᵐ Camden (Clarencieux). 16 Nov. 1623. Books (24 lines to a page : sometimes two titles to a line). 46ᵇ blank.
47. Rich. Burrell. 12 Nov. 1623. £10.
48. Dʳ David Dolben (afterwards Bp of Bangor). Two books.
Orlando Gibbons Organist of Sᵗ Peter's Church at Westminster (Speed's Chronicle and Book of Maps).
49. Dʳ Henry King (afterwards Bp of Chichester).
Dʳ Th. Mountford Archdeacon of Westminster. Complutensian Bible.
50. Dʳ Mountford President of Coll. of Physicians. 10 books.
51. Th. Morice. 2 vols.
Th. Peirce D.D. one of the Chaunters. Erasmus, 8 vols.
52. Jo. Wilson Dean of Rippon (preb.). 11 books.
53. Sʳ Arthur Ingram. 2 June 1624. £20.
54. Wᵐ Winne. 13 books.
55. Theod. Price D.D. (preb.). 16 May 1628. Bullarium, 3 vols.
56. Th. Hayne. 28 Sept. 1640. 7 vols.
Jo. King D.D. (preb.). 2 vols.
57. Rich. Owen. 14 Dec. 1624. 22 vols.
58. Jo. Pocklington D.D. 10 June 1624. £12.
59. Jo. Selden. (blank.)
60. Jo. Bill (King's Printer). 10 May 1624. More than 100 books.
63. Ric. Tufton. 4 July 1624. 17 books.
64. Valentine Moretoft. £10.
65. Lambert Osbaldston (preb.). Portrait of Williams which cost £25.
66. Th. Merill (Butler) by his Will. £5.
67. Ant. de Sousa Macedo. Portuguese ambassador. 2 books.
68. Jo. Spicer. 27 Aug. 1626. 4 books, and a great German Clock with a Chime (cf. *Munim.* 18,158 and 18,151).

[A clear change of hand here.]

69. Fran. Walsall D.D. (preb.). [Part of the Alcharon. Arab: MS.]
70. Edw. Fulliam (preb. of Windsor), Biblia Polyglotta (9 vols.) and Institution of the Garter.
71. Dʳ Jo. Dolben. Dean. 1663. 12 books, and
Missale vetus Pergam : olim Nichol. Lidlington Abbatis temp. Richardi secundi. Fol. MS. [The Litlington Missal.]
MS. Graece pergam. 4ᵒʳ Evangeliorum. ff. 72–3 blank.
74. Ric. Busby D.D. (preb. and schoolmaster). 1664. 15 books. f. 75 blank.

f. 76.	James Lamb D.D. (preb.).	1669.	11 books.	f. 77 blank.
78.	Wᵐ Hargwood D.D. (preb.).		£25.	f. 79 blank.
80.	Ric. Gowland (librarian).		£10.	
81.	Sam. Bolton D.D. (preb.).		5 books.	f. 82 blank.
83.	Th. Triplet D.D. (preb.).		26 books.	
85.	Herb. Thorndike (preb.).	1672.	Atlas (£55).	
86.	Walt. Jones D.D. (Subdean).		19 books.	
87.	Rich. Perrinchiefe D.D. (preb.).		8 vols.	

[At bottom ℞ Nov. 10. 1675 : then the hand changes.]

88.	Geo. Stradling Dean of Chichester (preb.).	10 vols.
89.	Laurence Earl of Rochester.	23 Jan. 1705. Clarendon's Hist. of Rebellion.
90.	Ch. Battely (receiver).	23 Ap. 1705. 1 vol.
91.	Sam. White (Fellow of Trinity).	„ „ „ 2 vols.
92.	Nic. Onely D.D. (preb.).	23 Jan. 1702. Life of Abp Williams.
93.	Jas. Wright.	„ „ 1692. 1 vol.

[Another hand : ornament ceases.]

94. Hen. Turner Clerk of the Parish of S. Margaret's. 1710. 12 books, and
Sʳ Edw. Walker's Journals MS. 1650.
Star Chamber MS.
Musick Book folio MS.
Combats and Challenges.

95. Bought with money from Stephen Fox and Christopher Wren Knights. 1709.
„ „ „ „ Th. Knipe (£10) S. Bradford (£10). 1710.

96.	Rich. Canning.	1712.
	Dʳ Broderick.	1713. £10.
	Dʳ South.	1715. His own works.

97. Dʳ Barton. Given by his widow. 24 Oct. 1718.
98. Other Prebendaries.
99. Given by Dʳ Only (preb.). 1725. 600 books.
Compendium Metaphysicum MS. [No. 32 in Catalogue.]
Liber MS. de Ecclesia Romana.
Dʳ Onley's Sermons 3 MS. Vols. in Quarto. [Not described : in a press
in the Library.]

107ᵇ	Dʳ Linford.	f. 108 blank.
109.	Bought. May 28. 1727.	
110.	Michael Evans (preb.). 1732. 200 books.	
	Gibbon's Divinity MS.	
113.	Bought. 1734.	
114.	Th. Moore (librarian). £50.	
114ᵇ.	Edw. Gee.	

Sʳ Th. Philips.
W. Morrice.
Ch. King.
Owen Davis Receiver.
The Crucified Jesus by Anth. Horneck D.D. a manuscript. [Extant :
not described.]
Simon Manningham.

Robt Freind D.D. Headmaster.

Martial's Epigramms a MS. [Either no. 15 or no. 16 in my catalogue.]

Hon. Rob. Drummond D.D. a Prebendary.

A drawing on vellum representing various things relating to Abbot Islip. [This is the Islip Roll, admirably published by W. H. St J. Hope, M.A., F.S.A., Hon. Secretary to the Society of Antiquaries, and recently returned by the Society to the Dean and Chapter.]

[This page is headed with the dates 1732 and 1747.]

115.　Bought.　　　　　　　1737.　1744.
116.　Bought.　　　　　　　1744.　1750.
　　　　　　　　　　　　　ff. 117—120 blank.

Then in the first hand (a new title-page) :

f. 121.　*A Catalogue of all such Manuscripts as have beene given to the Publicque Library at Westminster Togeither with the names of those which gave them.*

122.　The Right Honorable John Williams Doctor in Divinitie late ArchBpp of Yorke and Deane of Westminster sometimes Lord Keeper of ye Greate Seale of England and one of ye Privie Councillors to ye late King James and King Charles gave as followeth. viz :

[The grouping of the books under the numbers is necessarily conjectural in some cases.]

1, 2.　Biblia MS. Anglice 2^{obus} Vol. Fol.

3, 4.　*Pentateuchus Mosis Hebraice cum notis Massoreth : 2^{bs} Fol.

5.　*Biblia Hebraica MS. correctissima. Fol.

6.　Biblia Latine D. Hieronymi. Fol.

7.　Altera bellissimo charactere. Fol.

8.*　Altera una cum Indice plenissimo. Fol.

9.　A Summary of the whole Bible collected by John Wickleffe. 4to. (f. 122^b. Col. 1.)

10.　Liber Geneseos glossatus. Fol.

11.　Exodus glossat. Fol.

12.　Liber Levitici glossatus. Fol.

13.　Libri Numerorum et Deuteronomii glossati. Fol.

14.　Commentar. in Librum Job. Fol.

15.　Libri Joshuae et Judicum glossati. Fol.

16.　Libri 4^{or} Regum glossati. Fol.

17.　Glossa communis super Psalterium.

18.　Esajas Propheta glossatus.

19.　Hieremias et Baruch glossati.

20.　Paralippomenon libri duo. Proverbia et Ecclesiastes glossati. Fol.

21a.　Super Cantica et Apocalipsin. 8°.

　b.　De Lapidibus pretiosis eorumque virtutibus metrice.

[Space.]

(Col. 2.)

22.　Glossa super Ezechielem.

23.　super Danielem prophetam.

24. Matthaeus Evang: glossatus.
25. idem et Marcus glossati. 4to.
26. Lucas glossatus 4to.
27. Acta Apostolorum cum glossa. Fol.
28. D. Pauli Epistolae glossatae. Fol.
29. Catena Expositionum Patrum in D. Pauli Epistolas. Fol.
30. Liber Apocalypseos. Epistolae Canonicae et Actus Apostolorum glossat. Fol.
31. ⎰Commentarius in Apocalypsin. Fol.
    ⎱Aesopi Fabulae.

[Space.]

(Col. 1.)
32. Orthodoxographi. Fol.
33. Petrus Apollonius presbyter Novariensis in libellum de duello Davidis et Goliae, pulchro charactere, metrice.
34. Epistolae Ivonis Carnotensis. 4to. Origenes super Leviticum.

(Col. 2.)
35. Hugonis Parisiensis Didascalicon.
    Institutiones Novitiorum.
    De mundi contemptu.
    De arrha animae.
    De virginitate beatae Mariae.
    De potestate ligandi.
    De conjugio. Fol.

(f. 123. Col. 1.)
36. *Evangelium* D. Johannis carmine hexametro.
    De casibus conscientiae.
    Regulae monachorum.
37. D. Gregorii Moralia. Fol.
38. Augustinus de doctrina christiana.
    Sententiae Hugonis Parisiensis.
39. D. Gregorius in Ezechielem. 4to.
40. D. Chrysostomi Tractatus varii.
    Ambrosius de consecratione ecclesiae.
    Hug: archidiaconi ad Fulbertum Epistolae.
    Fulberti tractatus duo.
(41).*Psalmi Davidis.
    Hieronymus de viris illustribus.
    D. Augustini Tractatus varii una cum Prosperi ad eum Epistola.
    D. Hillarii Epistola ad Augustinum.
    Aug: de perseverantia Sanctorum.
42. D. Ambrosii Officia. 4to.
43. Isidorus Hispalensis super vetus Testamentum.
    Revelatio facta cuidam de 3^{bus} patriarchis.
44. Meditationes et Orationes valde utiles.
45. Isidori Hispalensis Commentar. in Pentateuchum Libri Josuae Iudicum et Regum.
    Augustinus de animae quantitate.
    Hieronym: in Actus Apostolorum.

46. Aug. de Charitate.
    Item de vita et moribus Clericorum.
47. D. Augustini Libri Confessionum 13^{cim} bellissimo charactere.
    (Col. 2.)
48. Idem de animae quantitate.
    Retractationes eiusdem.
49. D. Hieronymus contra Jovinianum.
    Eiusdem Epistola de Locis Mysticis.
    Augustinus adversus quinque Haereses.
50. Augustinus de Libero Arbitrio.
    Liber Ecclesiasticorum Dogmatum Gennadii.
    Fulgentii Epistola ad Donatum.
    Aug: de Penitentia.
    Abbas Cheremonensis (!) de perfectione.
    Aug: Tractatus aliqui.
51. Prosper de vita contemplativa. vetus Exemplar.
    De vitiis et virtutibus Libri 3^{es}.
    Cyprianus de opere et
    Augustinus de utilitate agendi Paenitentiam.
    Hugo Abbas de cohabitatione Fratrum.
    Aug: de laude et utilitate Canticorum Spiritualium.
52. Ivonis Carnotensis Epistolae, bello charactere. Fol.
53. Gregorii Nazianzeni Orationes interprete Ruffino.
54. Baeda in Epistolas Canonicas, pulchro charactere. Fol.
55. Chrysostomi Homiliae. 8º.
56. Alcuinus presbyter de virtutibus et vitiis.
    Vita S. Euphrasiae.
    Passio S. Julianae Virginis et Martyris.
    Monita D. Basilii.
    Anonymus de virtutibus et vitiis.
    Epigramata quaedam a S^{to} Bonifacio missa ad sororem suam.
    (f. 123^b. Col. 1.)
    B. Ambrosius de Mysteriis.
    Fragmenta Librorum eiusdem de Sacramentis.
57. Postilla super Cantica Cantic: Salom:
    Item super Lam: Jeremiae.
    Sermones Dominicales.
    Summa Roberti Grosthead Lincoln. Ep.
    Tabula, et Excerpta Rabani de Etymologiis.
    Didascalicon Hugonis de S^{to} Victore.
    Aug: de spiritu et anima.
    Itinerarium mentis in Deum per Bonaventuram.
    Summa de Anima.
    Meditationes Bernardi.
    Id: de 12^m gradibus scalae Iacob.
    Apologeticum cuiusdam ad Fratres Cluniacenses.
    Hugo de Instructione Novitiorum.
    Notabilia Magistralia super Esajam. Fol.
58. Balduinus Ep. Wigorniensis de Sacramentis.

59. Eiusdem sermones de Commendatione Fidei.
    Item varii tractatus Theologici.
60a. Roberti Grosthead Ep. Linc. Epistolae et Sermones.
  b. Eiusdem allegationes pro Statu Ecclesiae coram papa et cardinalibus
      A° D^{ni} 1250 etc. Fol.
  c. Idem in 1^{mam} 2^{dae}. 4to.
  d. Eiusdem summa Philosophiae. 4to
61. Regula S^{ti} Benedicti.
    Martyrologium Romanum.
    Evangelia et Epistolae.
  (Col. 2.)
62. Alexandri Neckam opus Magnum de Naturis Rerum. Fol.
    Eiusdem in Ecclesiasten Commentarius.
    Item Psalmi Davidis.
63. Petri Lombardi Sententiae cum notis passim. Fol.
64. D. August: Sermones. Fol.
65. Expositio Vocabulorum S. Bibliae.
    Item Dictionarium Latino-Anglic: vet.
66. Liber Scintillarum, pulchro charactere.
67. Sermones Quinquagesimales.
68. ⎰Lucerna Conscientiae anonymi cuiusdam.
    ⎱Innocentius de miseria conditionis humanae.
69. ⎰Rich. de S^{to} Victore de Benjamin et fratribus eius.
    ⎱Augustinus de Gratia Novi Testamenti.
70. Aug: de singularitate clericorum.
    Item de sermonibus Domini in Monte.
    Epistola Excusatoria Origenis.
    Hieronym: de honorandis parentibus.
    Aug: de Agone Christiano.
    Hieronymi ad Principiam virg: Epistola.
    Aug: super Epist: Canon: Johannis.
    Epistolae Baedae ad Egbertum Ep^{m}.
    Hugo de 3^{bus} silentiis.
    Sermo Bernardi de Custodia cordis.
    Aug: de serm: Christi in monte.
    Athanasius de miraculis per imaginem Crucifixi.
    Id: de confessione et obedientia.
    Dialogus Pastoralium D. Chrysostomi.
    Id: de Laude crucis.
    Id: de Johanne Baptista.
  (f. 124. Col. 1.)
    De ascensione Christi ad caelum.
    De muliere Chananaea.
    Ambrosius de 3^{bus} Difficilibus.
    Bern: de memoria novissimorum.
    Idem de triplici amore.
    De cautela humanae laudis recipiendae.
    Aug: de vita Christiana.
    Id: de Corde (Corpore) et Sanguine domini.

Aug: alia.

Leo de Redemptione Hominis.

Capitula quaedam ex libro Prosperi de vita contemplativa.

Epistola Aug: ad Quod Vult Deus.

Aug: de Haeresibus.

Sermones Lincolniensis.

Wallensis de Paenitentia eiusque partibus.

D. Basilius super 1^{mum} versic: psalmi 1^{mi}.

Sermo Bernardi in Dominicam 1^{mam} in Adventu.

Alter eiusd: in obitu Humberti.

71.
- Tractatus de Instructione Praelatorum in arte Medicinae Spiritualis pertinentis ad regimen animarum. 4to
- Libellus de doctrina cordis.
- Columba Noae.
- De antichristo.

72.
- De miseria humanae conditionis.
- De instabilitate mundi.
- De morte corporis.
- De die Judicii.
- De Poenis Inferni et Gaudiis Caeli. Anglice.
- The Passion of Christ according to ye 4 Evangelists.

(Col. 2.)

73. Vita Mariae Aegyptiacae Authore Sophronio Hieros:

Vita S^{tae} Mariae (Marinae) virginis.

B. Ephraim de Compunctione, de Die Judicii, de Resurrectione et Regno Caelorum. Fol.

74. *Petri Lombardi sententiae. 4to.

75.
- Almansoris Opera Physica, de Arabico in Latin: translata. Fol.
- Verba Abbuteti sive Antidotarium.

76. Hippocratis Aphorismi.

Theophilus de Urinis.

Viaticum, sive tractatus de morbis eorumque curatione. Fol.

Bern: Alfani Archiep: Liber aureus de Medicina: de vino, urinis, inspectione sanguinis et phlebotomia per Ric. Anglicum.

77. De re Medica scriptores varii: Fol.

78. Isaac de Diaetis.

Glossa super Regimen Galieni Liber.

It: de Febribus cum aliis. 4to.

79.
- Bern: de Gordonio Regimen Sanitatis.
- Eiusd: Libri prognostici.
- Id: de regimine morborum acutorum.
- Antidotarium Nicholai.
- Bernardi de graduatione.
- Id: in tractatu de phlebotomia.
- Anatomia Guidonis.
- De medicinis componendis.
- De Dosibus.
- Brevis tr: Arnoldi de phlebotomia.
- Id: in tr: de multiplici uno.
- Tr. de modo medendi secundum Gerardum.

(f. 124 *b*. Col. 1.)

80.
- Varii tractatus Chymici.
- De calcinatione Saturni et Jovis.
- Elixar Lunae super Venerem.
- ⊙ quomodo fit ex ♀.
- Morienus Mulaphary de speculo alchimiae.
- Liber vet: philosophorum de proprietatibus Rerum.
- Morienus ad Flodiu^~: ? Flodium.
- Idem de Expos: Lap: benedicti.
- Hermes de transmutatione metallorum.
- Arnold: Villanovanus, Ioseph: Baco: Ortolong.
- Merlinus metrice.
- Senior sive clavis sapientiae minoris.

81. Passionarium Galieni. 4to.

82.
- Joh: a S^to Amando super antidotarium Nicholai. 4to.
- Abbreviarium Hippocratis super Regimen Febrium acutarum etc.

83. Avicennae opera. Fol.

84. Ioh: Platearii Glossa in antidotarium Nicholai.

85. D. Iustiniani Codex de Trinitate et Fide Catholica cum comment. Fol.

(Col. 2.)

86. Eiusdem ex omni vet: jure. Digestum seu Pandectae. Fol.
Gul. de Mandagoto Archid: Nemausensis de Electionibus.

87. Gul. de Pagula de Oculo Sacerdotis dextro et sinistro.

88. Compendium vitae spiritualis. 8°.
Thomae Claxton cantus comicus.

89. Decreta Ecclesiastica Ecclesiarum orbis Britannici pam-Britannica pan-Anglica, provincialia, Dioecesana, ab initio Relig: Christianae ad ann: Christi 1222. Fol.

90. Chronica Martini paenitentiarii Papae. Fol.

91. Statuta Roberti de Winchelsey Archiep. Cant. in Consistorio de Arcubus.
Statuta Synodalia praesidente Nicholao Ep. Wintoniensi.
Acta Concilii Londini celebrati praesidente Othone Cardinale Sedis Apostol: Legato.
Acta Concilii sub Octoboni praesidentia una cum adjectionibus.
Concilium Lambethanum praesidente Joh. de Peckham Cant. Archiep.
Statuta Synodalia Richardi Cicestrensis Ep.

(f. 125. Col. 1.)
Statuta Gilberti Cicestrensis Ep. a° Dñi 1292.
Constitutiones Epp. totius Angliae apud Merton.
Constitutiones Simonis de Mepham Londini Anno. 1328.
Mandagotus.

92. Perspectiva Alhazen Libris 7^m Fol.

93. Julius Firmicus de Mathesi, bello charactere, fol.

94. Joh. de Sacrobosco Computus, de sphaera, etc. 8°

95, 6, 7. Titi Livii Opera 3^bus [voll.] pulcherrimo charactere conscripta.

98. Xenophontis Historia de vita Cyri. 4to.

99. Diodori Siculi Libri aliquot Latinitate donati a Poggio Florentino pulchro charactere. Fol.

100. Trogus Pompeius bellissimo charactere.

101. Aemil: Probus de ducibus nationum exterarum praeclaris.
     Chronologia Imperatorum Rom: ab Octaviano ad Fred: 2^dum.
102. Plinius de viris illustribus.
     De vitis Imperatorum. Luc. Florus.
     Evidentia Tragaediarum Senecae.
     Corvinus Messala ad Octavianum Caesarem de progenie sua et de urbis
     Romae originibus.
103. Orationes variae excerptae ex Livio Curtio Salustio aliisque. 4to

(Col. 2.)

104. {Lupis in Xenophontis praefectum equitum etc.
     {Ioh. Argyropilus de Laudibus Scientiae. 4to.
105. Analytica Aristotelis priora et posteriora Graece. 4to.
106. Platonis Phaedon et alia. Fol.
107. Translatio Oeconomicorum Aristotelis cum Explicatione in usum Cosmae
     de Medicis.
108. Anastasii λόγοι δώδεκα Graece. Fol.
109. {Πλατων περὶ ὅρων περὶ ἀρετῆς καὶ θανάτου.
     {'Αριστοτέλης περὶ 'Αρετῶν. 4to
110. Crispi Salustii Bellum Catalinarium.
111. Alter.
112. Valerii Maximi Dicta et Facta Memorabilia, bello charactere. 4to
113. Auli Gellii Noctes Atticae. Fol.
114. Terentii Comoediae etc.
115. Donati Grammatici Comentarii super Terentii Comoedias.
116. Terentius alter. 12mo.
117. {Valerii Maximi Dicta et Facta Memorabilia.
     {Palladius Rutilus de re Rustica.
     {D. Augustinus de Natura Boni.
118. Boetius de consolatione vet.
119. Doctrinale per Giovanni Dominici Ital. 4to.

(f. 125*b*. Col. 2.)

120. Lepidi Comici Philodoxios Fabulae.
121. *Guarini Veronensis Epistolae ad Chrisoloram aliosque. 4to
122. Joh: Bapt: Evangelistae Orationes et poemata Latine et(c) Italice. 4to
123. Isotae Nogarolae Epistolae ad varios Italos magni nominis.
     Petri Parleonis apologia pro milite qui hostem iniussu Ducis eius aggressus
     est.
124. {Pindari Olympia Pythia etc. Graece.
     {Adagiarium.
     {Zenobii Epitome Tarraei et Dydimi. 4to.
125. *{Γνῶμαι μονοστοχαί (μονοστιχοι) ex variis Poetis.
     {Callimachi Hymni.
126. Virgilii Bucolica Georgica Aeneis etc. bello charactere. 4to
127. Virgilii Aeneis vetustiss: Exemplari.
     Eius Eclogae.
128. Ovidii Epistolae.
     Ovidius de arte amandi.
129. Q. Horatius cum commentario amplo.
130. Alter. 4to

131. Eius Epistolae cum notis. 4to.
132. Tibulli poemata bello charactere. 4to.
133. Epistolae. 4to.
134. Junii Juvenalis Satyrae.
C. Plinii 2^di Epistolae bello charactere.

(Col. 2.)
135. Senecae Tragaediae cum annotat: exemplar vetus. 4to.
136. Lucani Pharsalia pulchro charactere. 4to.
137. Claudianus cum variis antiq: manuscriptis collatus.
138. Apollinaris Sidonii Panegyres et Epistolae.
139. Lucani Fragmenta.
140. Eman: Moscopulus περὶ τῆς τῶν ὀκτὼ τοῦ λόγου μερῶν διορθώσεως.
141. Hermogenes cum scholiis Graece vet. Fol.
142. Pompeius Festus de significantiis.
143. Dictionarium. 4to.
Eiusdem Doctrina Compendiosa per literas.
144. Nonius Marcellus de proprietatibus et differentiis sermonis Latini.
145. Εξήγησις περὶ ψυχῆς. Fol.
145a. Ammonii 'Εξήγησις περὶ κατηγοριῶν Gr. (?) in folio.
Alexander Aphrodisiensis Gr. (?) περὶ τῶν 'Αναλυτικῶν.
146. Poggius Florentinus in Luciani Asinum ab eod: Latinitate donatum.
147. Galfridi Monemuthensis Historia Britannica.
Turpinus Archiep: Rhemensis de Carlo Magno.
148. Giraldi Cambrensis descriptio Walliae. 4to.

(126. Col. 1.)
149. Historia Angliae incipiens Britannia et desinens circa initium H^ci 6^ti.
150. Benedictus Abbas de gestis Henrici 2^ndi Regis Angliae.
151. *Burchiello sonetti sopra diversi occasione.

(Col. 2.)
152. Historia Angliae vetus incipiens a Bruto.
153. S. Oswaldi Regis et Martyris Vita et Commemoratio.
154. Dante delle diversi cerchie del infierno et paradiso, vet.

(Col. 1.)
155. *Gospells for everie Sunday. Italice. Fol.
156. A new Testament. 12mo vetus.
157. Psalmi Davidis cum variis canticis sacris. 4to.
158. A Hieroms Bible in a very old character. 8vo
159. Precationes et Hymni. 12mo.
160. *A Divine History of some Famous English Divines metrice.
161. An old Missall, folio.
162. Certaine Psalmes translated into English Rithme by William Forest, in imitation of xx^tie formerlie presented to H^y ye 8th by Sr Thomas Sternhold for Q. Katherine.
163. *Certaine Commonplaces of Divinitie scholastically translated. Also diverse Sermons. Latine. 4to.
164. An Exposicion of the tenn Commandements. 4to.
165. A Treatise that may suffice each man & woman to live by wherein is an Exposicion of the Creede Tenn Commandements etc. 12mo.

166. *A right Learning to know a man's selfe, by the consideracion of the present and the time to come. 4to.
167. *The Life of Christ with some Colleccions out of Bernard.
    S^{ti} Francisci Vita etc. 3^{bus} comprehensa libris. 8vo.
168. *A little Manuall. 24to.

(Col. 2.)
169. Of the tenn Commandements and the Exposition of them.
    Of the Seven deadly sins. Of Faith: Hope: and Charity.
    Certaine Direccions of Godlie Liveing to Kings Priests Lords and Labourors:
    in speciall, how each man should be saved in his degree. 8^{uo}.
    Of men's worshipping Images, other wayes than Gods Law saies they should.
    How to know Antichrist and his many from Christ and his Followers.
    The Sisters and Bretheren.
    Augustine to an Earle.
170. {Summa Magistri Thomae Archidiaconi Sarum. 4to vet.
     {Certaine psalmes.
171. Arch. Bpp Cranmer his answere to the Sophistick cavillacions of Steph:
    Gardiner Bpp. of Winchester against the true doctrine of the Holy
    Sacram^{t} together with his answere to such places of Doct^{r}: Rich: Smith
    as deserve it.
    A coppie also of Gardiner's Booke that he presented in open Court. Italice.

(126^{b} Col. 1.)
172. *Letters Quadripartite Betweene King Henry the 7th, John Islip Abbott of
    Westm: the Deane and Chapter of St Paul. London, the Major of
    London and the Commonaltie That the said Abbott paying the said
    Deane & Chapter such a sum as is there mencioned, they the said
    Deane etc. shall yearly on a sett day celebrate an Anniversary in theire
    Church for the said King his Praedecessors, himselfe. his Queene etc. in
    Blew velvet & gilt clasps.

(Col. 2.)
173. *Another Coppie of the like quadripartite Indenture Betweene the King y^{e}
    Abbott of Westm: Major of London & ye Deane & Chapt^{r} of St Stephens
    For the like Anniversary for the same End to be solemnized by them. Fol.
174. *King H. ye 8th his Erection of the Church of Westm: into a Bpprick etc.
    wth ye concessions he made unto the Bpp. thereof etc. Alsoe Queene
    Elizabeth her lettres Pattents whereby she made the said Church
    collegiate appointing there a Deane twelve Prebendaryes etc. Fol.
    f. 127 *is blank*.
    f. 128. Sr Robert Cotton Knight & Baronet gave these Manuscripts hereafter
    following:

Col. 1.
175. 1. Robertus Grostheed Lincolniensis Ep^{us} de Oculo Morali.   (Otho D. x.)
    Id: de Dispositione Motoris et Moti in motu circulari.
    Dictamina sive Lecturae eiusd: 147.
    Descriptio Figurae Machinae mundi.
    Id: de Cessatione Legalium.
    De conceptione b^{tae} Mariae secundum Anselmum.
    Expositio Prologi D. Hieronymi super Bibliam.

Col. 2.

176. 2. Historia quaedam de Regno Angliae et Regibus eius. (Otho D. xi.)
item de Paschae observatione in Anglia et de primis Regalibus orna-
mentis Regni Angliae.

Genealogia D^{ni} Petri de Luxemburg Comitis S^{ti} Pauli.

Item Genealogia D^{nae} Margaritae uxoris eius.

LOffice de seneschal, de Bailif et plusieurs autres officiers. Gallice.

128b. Col. 1.

Tractatus de re rustica. Gallice.

De cure(-a) Rei Familiaris ad Comitissam Nicholae per Rob. Grosseteste.

De arte culinaria veteri ubi elucidantur vocabula Ferculorum quae
habentur in prandiis Coronationum et Installationum. Gall.

Liber de Gemmis pretiosis et Herbis Salutaribus. Gallice.

Decimae triennales.

Antiqua Taxatio Beneficiorum appropriatorum et nova, cum Foedis
Militum et Donationibus spectantibus ad quaedam Monasteria in
Comitatu Eboracensi.

Prophetia de iis quae contingerent ad Annum D^{ni} 1290 inter Germanos
Italos Gallos Anglos Wallos et Scotos.

Literae Edwardi 3^{tii} Reg: Angli universis declarantes injurias sibi illatas
a Philippo Valesio Rege Franciae.

Literae Benedicti Papae ad Edu: Reg: Angl: de causa inter papatum et
Ludov: de Bavaria Imperatorem.

Eiusd: Literae ad Eund: de componenda pace inter Reges Edv: et
Philippum.

Edvardi Reg: Literae ad Collegium Cardinalium, et univers: Ecclesiarum
praelatos de eadem materia.

Col. 2.

De ead: Controversia Literae patentes ad universos Reges etc.

Mutuae Literae Ludovici Imp. Romanorum et Edv: Regis Angliae de
eadem etc.

Roberti Grosseteste Ep: Lincoln: sermones.

Variae eius Orationes Romae habitae etc.

Id: de Libero Arbitrio. Fol.

A French Romance of his, in the Titel whereof hee is called Bpp. of
Nicholle. 4to

177. 3. Roberti Ep. Lincoln: Epistola Monitoria ad Priorem et conventum de
Newham. (Otho C. xv.)

Visitatio eiusd: domus per Archidiac: Lincoln ex authoritate D^{ni} Papae
A^o 1232.

Consultatio de cohibendis Tartarorum incursionibus per processus,
ieiunia etc.

Regulae S^{ti} Augustini de vita Clericorum.

Ordinatio Canonicorum Regularium.

Rituale, sive Consuetudinarium.

Fragmentum Homiliae Saxonicae.

Ordo Conversorum.

Mandagotus de Electionibus faciendis.

Grosseteste de 7^m Sacramentis.

De Inventione Musicae per sonum malleorum super incudem.
Tractatus de periculis quae accidunt circa officium sacerdotis.

129 a. Col. 1.

178. 4. Calendarium Rerum in Anglia gestarum.   (Otho C. xvi.)
Extractum Chronicarum Rogeri Cestrensis.
Vita Roberti Grosseteste Linc. Ep^i per Ricardum Monachum Bardinensis
Caenobii.
Martyrium S^{ti} Hugonis Ep^i (!) Lincoln:
Rogerus Dimmocke contra errores Lollardorum.
Passio S^{ti} Kenelmi Regis.

Col. 2.

De S^{to} Edwardo Rege et Martyre.
De S^{to} Guthlaco Heremita.
Vita S^{ti} Elphegi Archiep^i.
Vita Sancti Johannis Beverlacensis.
Historia Joh^{is} Beverlaci per Folchard: Monachum Dorobernens:
Constitutiones Eboracensis Ecclesiae A^o 1291.
A sermon in Defence of the Holy Scriptures, in English.

ff. 129—140 are blank.

C.

Librorum Manuscriptorum Ecclesiae Westmonasteriensis Catalogus. (ii. 27.)
Colligit autem ille bonae notae Codices ccxxx.
Accurante vero (viro) erudito Michaele Ma(i)ttaerio.

1091. 1. Menologium Graecum.
    2. Martyrologium Graecum cum orationibus aliquot. SS. Patrum.
    3. Commentarius in Epistolas S. Pauli. Gr.
    4. Georgii Codini Origines Constantinopolitanae. Gr.
    5. Aristotelis organon. Gr.
    6. Joannes Grammaticus de anima. Gr.
    7. Anastasii orationes 12. Gr.
    8. Commentarius in Aristotelis Logicam, viz. Ammonii, Michaelis Patricii,
        Alexandri Aphrodisiensis etc. Gr.
    9. Disputatio Coresii contra Cornelium Pisanum Praelectorem de
        Monarchia Ecclesiastica. Gr.
1100. 10. Galenus $\pi\epsilon\rho\grave{\iota}$ $\kappa\rho\acute{\iota}\sigma\epsilon\omega\nu$.
    11. Aphthonii Progymnasmata cum Scholiis: et Hermogenis Rhetorica.
        Gr. p. 61 (*sic*).
    12. Platonis $\acute{o}\rho o\iota$.
    13. Moschopuli Grammatica. Gr.
    14. Idem $\pi\epsilon\rho\grave{\iota}$ $\sigma\chi\epsilon\delta\tilde{\omega}\nu$.
    15. Pindari Olympia, Pythia, Nemea. Gr.

16. Nonius Marcellus.
17. Priscianus.
18. Alius.
19. Pompeius Festus.
1110. 20. Alius.
21. Perspectiua Alhacen lib. 7.
22. An. Senecae Tragoediae.
23. Eaedem.
24. Terentius.   25. Idem.
26. Horatii Opera.
27. Eiusdem Epistolae quaedam et Ars Poetica.
28. Eiusdem Odae cum veteris commentatoris notis.
29. Vi(r)gilii Opera.
30. Eiusdem Aeneis.
1121. 31. Justinus Historicus.
32. Sallustius.
33. Lucani quaedam.
34. Juvenalis Satyrae et Plinii Epistolae.
35. 35 (*sic*) Plinii Epistolae: et Vita B. Pauli primi Eremitae per Hiero-
nymum.
36. Hieronymus de Viris illustribus.
37. Orationes excerptae ex Historicis Latinis.
38. Ovidii Epistolae et Ciceronis Timaeus de essentia mundi.
*39. Eclogae Petrarchae.
Statii et Claudiani quaedam.
1130. *40. Poemata Tavolae.
41. B. Prosper de vita contemplativa et activa.
Cyprianus de Opere et Eleëmosyna.
Augustinus de utilitate agendae Poenitentiae.
Sermo Hugonis de cohabitatione Fratrum.
Augustinus de utilitate spiritualium Canticorum.
42. Donatus in 5 priores Fabulas Terentii.
43. Xenophontis Cyropaedia et Platonis Gorgias, Lat.
44. Sidonii Apollinaris Poemata et Epistolae.
45. T. Livii Decas prima.   46. Eiusdem decas tertia.
47. Eiusdem decas quarta.
48. Valerius Maximus.
49. Asinus Luciani. / Xenophontis ἵππαρχος / Isocratis Demonicus / Luciani
quaedam. Lat.
1140. 50. Ciceronis Officia.
51. Poemata Latina Baptistae Mantuani.
52. Comoedia Philodoxii et Epistolae quaedam.
53. Plinius de Viris illustribus / L. Florus /. Evidentia tragoediarum
Senecae /
Corvinus Messala ad Octavianum Caesarem Augustum de progenie
sua et Romae regiminibus.
54. De re oeconomica.
55. Vi(r)gilii Eclogae / Sallustius / Epistola Sapphus / Hieronymus ad
Nepotianum.

56. Tibullus.   57. Alius.
58. Ovidius de arte amandi.
59. Lucanus.
1150. 60. Sallustius.
61. Epistola Nogarolae et ad Nogarolam. / Oratio ad Legatos Venetos.
Oratio Petri Parleonis pro milite qui iniussu Imperatoris egressus
fudit hostes / Vita Homeri.
62. Poemata Petri Apollonii Presbyteri Novariensis.
*63. J. Fleete de Fundatione et Dedicatione Ecclesiae Westmonasteriensis.
64. A. Gellius.   65. Alius.
66. Diodori Siculi libri quidam. Lat.
67. Tractatus super Apocalypsin / Aesopi Fabulae, Lat.
68. Platonis Phaedon et Callicles. Lat.
*69. Terentius.
1160. *70. MSS. Arab. viz., Solutio Aenigmatum / Praeceptio de vita pia / oratio
de consolatione.
71. Liber Missalis.
72. Comedie di Dante D'Algieri, viz. Inferno, Purgatorio, Cielo.
73. Liber Missalis.   74. Alius.   75. Alius.
76. Officia quaedam Romana viz. B. Virginis.
77. Liber Precum.   78. Alius.   79. Orationes Divinae.
1170. 80. Ordo ad faciendam Aquam Benedictam / ordo Commendationis animae /
ordo ad faciendum Baptismum.
81. A godly Book, containing rules for each man and woman to live after.
82. Novum Testamentum, seu Historia Evangelica.
83. Psalterium Latinum.   84. Aliud.
85. An English New Testament.   86. Another.
87. Les Evangiles.
88. Les Actes et Epistres des Apostres.
*89. Evangelia Graece.
1180. 90. Homiliae Joannis Chrysostomi, Lat.
91. Hieronymus contra Jovinianum / Eiusdem Epistola de locis mysticis /
Augustinus contra 5 Haereses.
92. Ambrosius de Officiis.
93. Moralia Gregorii.
94. Gregorii Nazianzeni Orationes quaedam. Lat.
95. Beda in Epistolas SS. Jacobi, Petri, Johannis et Judae.
96. Gregorius Papa in Ezechielem.
97. Liber Sententiarum.
98. Liber Summarum.
99. Isidorus Hispalensis in Vetus Testamentum.
1190. 100. Isidorus in Pentateuchum, Josuam, Judices, et Reges.
Augustinus de Animae quantitate: et eiusdem Retractationes.
Hieronymus in Acta Apostolorum.
101. Augustini Sermones.
102. Eiusdem de Animae quantitate et Retractationes.
103.   „   de Civitate dei.
104.   „   de gratia Novi Testamenti.
105.   „   de libero arbitrio.

106. Eiusdem confessiones.
107.   „   de Charitate.
*108.   „   contra Felicianum Haereticum.
109.   „   de doctrina Christiana / Sententiae Hugonis Parisiensis.
1200. *110. Expositiones in Evangelia Festorum.
111. Tabula Dictorum Domini Lincolniensis.
112. Homiliae quaedam Hisp*anice*.
113. Alcuinus de Virtutibus / Vita Euphrasiae / Passio Julianae / Monitor Basilii / Epigrammata Bonifacii / Ambrosius de Mysteriis.
114. Lucerna Conscientiae / Innocentius de miseria humana.
115. Apparatus in processu in ordine Justiciario.
116. Of the Ten Commandments and the Seven Deadly Sins.
117. Gulielmi de Pagula Oculus dexter et sinister Sacerdotis.
118. A Dialogue between a Preacher and a Romish Priest.
119. A Book of Divine Poems.
1210. 120. Liber Scintillarum.
121. Baldwinus de Commentatione Fidei.   122. Idem de Sacramento Altaris.
123. Tractatus Divini qui incipiunt: *Ubi erat deus antequam esset creatura.*
124. Hugonis Parisiensis Didascalicon, Isagoge, Institutiones Novitiorum, etc.
125. Alexander Necham de rerum naturis / Psalmorum liber.
126. Josephus, Latine.   127. Alius.
128. Codex Juris cum glossis.
129. Expositiones SS. Patrum in Biblia, viz. Dionysii, Ignatii, Polycarpi, Iustini, etc.
1220. 130. Tractatus Diversorum Patrum, Augustini, Origenis, Hieronymi, etc.
131. Expositio Alphabetica Vocabulorum Biblicorum.
132. Epistolae Ivonis.
133. Epistolae Ivonis / Origenes in Leviticum / Psalterium B. Mariae.
134. Oswaldi Regis et Martyris Vita.
135. Institutio Praelatorum in arte Medicinae Spiritualis.
136. Capita Evangeliorum metrice / Summa Casuum.
137. An Exposition on the Decalogue.
138. Piorum Picorumque monumenta Genealogica.
139. Meditationes et orationes utiles.
1230. 140. Compendium Vitae Spiritualis / Modus Confitendi / Speculum S Edmundi.
141. Summa Magistri Thomae.
142. Regula S. Benedicti / Martyrologium Romanum.
143. De miseria humanae conditionis / De morte corporis.
144. Tractatus Theologici, Postillae, et Sermones.
145. Stephani, Bonifacii, Othoboni, Archiepisc. Cant. Constitutiones.
146. Valerius Maximus / Palladius de agricultura. Augustinus de natura Boni / De opere monachorum.
147. Tractatus varii Joannis Episcopi, Ambrosii, Hugonis, Fulberti, etc.
*148. Liber S. Edmundi Regis.
149. Liber Somniorum per Galfridum de Monmouth editus sub nomine Turpini.

1240. 150. Almanzor, Lat.
151. Sermones quidam Latini.
152. Joannes de S. Amando.
153. Liber Medicinae. 154. Alius. 155. Alius.
156. Avicenna, Lat.
157. De re medica scriptores varii.
158. Liber medicinae.
159. Bernardus de Medicamentis.
1250. 160. Bernardus de regimine Morborum.
161. Tractatus varii de Chemica.
162. Bernardi regimen Sanitatis.
163. Julii Materni Firmici libri Matheseos.
164. Liber Astronomicarum Observationum. 165. Alter hujusmodi.
166. Chronologia Imperatorum Romanorum.
167. Liber de re Medica.
168. Herbaticum Dioscorides de Herbis Faeminis.
169. Descriptio Cambriae.
1260. 170. Historia Britonum.
171. Chronicon S. Albani: incipit: *Britannia quae nunc dicitur Anglia* etc.
172. Passionarium.
173. Decreta Ecclesiastica Ecclesiarum orbis Britannici, per H. Spelman.
174. Notationes in omnes Paulinas Epistolas, una cum Prologo B. Hieronymi.
175. S. Biblia Latina. 176. Eadem.
177, 178. An English Bible. 2. vol.
179. The Summary of the whole Bible.
1271. 180. Glossae in Epistolas Pauli.
181. Danielem. 182. Iosuam.
183. Genesin. 184. Exodum.
185. Numeros. 186. Jobum.
187. Leviticum. 188. Reges.
189. Psalterium. **1280.** 190. Paralipomena, Proverbia, Ecclesiasten.
1281. 191. Isaiam. 192. Psalterium.
193. Jeremiam. 194. Ezechielem.
195. Matthaeum. 196. Matthaeum et Marcum.
197. Lucam. 198. Actus Apostolorum.
199. Apocalypsin, Epistolas, Actus. **1290.** 200. Apocalypsin.
1291. *201. A great Folio of old English Poems.
*202. Another, lesser.
203. Summa Philosophiae, per Grostead.
*204. NOMOTEXNIA, or the Art of Law.
*205. Tractatus Theologici.
206. Vita Mariae Ægyptiacae et S. Marinae Virginis. B. Ephrem de compunctione.
*207. Tractatus Philosophici.
*208. Summa Legum per Andream Horne.
*209. De Heroibus Israelis. Metrice.
1300. 210. Una Risposial del Reverend Padre Thomaso Cranmero.

211. Boethius.
*212. Historiae Britannicae defensio per Jo. Priscum (Priseum) Britannum.
213. An English Manuscript of Divinity.
*214. A Catalogue of persons outlaw'd in King *James's* Reign.
*215. A Collection of several Pleas and Demurs of certain Parliament-men.
*216. The Copies of such Records as upon search were brought in Parliament, 7 Jac. I.
217. Concerning several Offices: as of Seneschal, Bailiff, etc.
*218. A Folio Book of Miscellanies which begins, *Jus legationis* etc.
*219. Several Letters, *French* and *Latin*, of *Casimir, Mercier, Clervant, de la Tour*, etc.
1310. *220. Eight several Grants to Abbots of *Westminster*.
*221. Juramenta, sive onera officiariorum.
*222. Orders conceived and set down by Sir *Humphry May*.
*223. Modus tenendi Parliamentum.
*224. A Law Book of the Term S. Trin. 15 Jac.
225. Some Psalms in *English* Verse by W. *Forest*.
*226. Martyrologio de Santi del Signiore, etc.
*227. Statuta edita a confratribus B. Mariae observanda in honorem conceptionis.
*228. A Survey of the Archbishop of *Canterbury*.
*229. De Dei Scientia.
1320. *230. A Book of Acts and other Passages in Parliament.

COMPARATIVE TABLE OF THE THREE LISTS.

A. 1.	B. vac.	C. 3.
A. 2.	B. vac.	C. 9.

Probably the dialogue περὶ τῆς ἀρχῆς τοῦ Πάπα mentioned in Fabricius *Bibl. Gr.* XII. 118.

A. 3.	B. vac.	C. 2.
A. 4.	B. vac.	C. 4.

Edited by Lambecius 1655 etc., and in the various editions of the Byzantine historians.

A. 5.	B. vac.	C. 10.
A. 6.	B. vac.	C. 1.
A. 7.	B. 141.	C. 11.
A. 8.	B. 145ᵃ	C. 8.
A. 9.	B. 145.	C. 6.

Joh. Philoponus: often edited.

A. 10.	B. 108.	C. 7.

Fabr. *Bibl. Gr.* X. 589.

A. 11.	B. 109.	C. 12.

περὶ ἀρετῆς, a spurious dialogue: περὶ θανάτου = Axiochus.

A. 12.	B. 140.	C. 13.

Fabr. *Bibl. Gr.* VI. 322.

A.	13.	B.	105.	C.	5.
A.	14.	B.	vac.	C.	14.

Fabr. *Bibl. Gr.* VI. 324.

A.	15.	B.	124.	C.	15.

For Zenobii Epitome etc. see Fabr. *Bibl. Gr.* V. 109.

A.	16.	B.	vac.	C.	17.
A.	17.	B.	vac.	C.	18.
A.	18.	B.	144.	C.	16.
A.	19.	B.	142.	C.	19.
A.	20.	B.	143.	C.	20.
A.	21–23.	B.	95–97.	C.	45–47.
A.	24.	B.	115.	C.	42.
A.	25.	B.	135.	C.	22.
A.	26.	B.	vac.	C.	23.
A.	27.	B.	131.	C.	27.
A.	28.	B.	126 (or 127ᵃ).	C.	29.
A.	29.	B.	127 (127ᵃ) or 126.	C.	30?

There is some difficulty in distinguishing the various copies of Virgil in these lists.

A.	30.	B.	129.	C.	28.
A.	31.	B.	130.	C.	26.
A.	32.	B.	134.	C.	34.
A.	33.	B.	101.	C.	37.
A.	35.	B.	128.	C.	38.
A.	36.	B.	110.	C.	32.
A.	37.	B.	139?	C.	33?
A.	38.	B.	vac.	C.	vac.
A.	39.	B.	vac.	C.	vac.

Probably a quite late MS.

A.	40.	B.	138.	C.	44.
A.	41.	B.	106.	C.	68.
A.	42.	B.	vac.	C.	35.
A.	43.	B.	100.	C.	31.
A.	44.	B.	113.	C.	64.
A.	45 (in Harl. 694).	B.	vac.	C.	65.
A.	46.	B.	cf. 101.	C.	36.

Aemilius Probus is the book now known as Cornelius Nepos.

A.	47.	B.	98.	C.	43.
A.	48.	B.	102.	C.	53.

Corvinus Messala : this tract is a forgery of the Italian Revival. It is sometimes printed with Eutropius.

A.	49.	B.	99.	C.	66.
A.	50.	B.	112.	C.	48.
A.	51.	B.	146.	C.	49.
A.	52.	B.	vac.	C.	50.
A.	53.	B.	vac.	C.	vac.
A.	54.	B.	vac.	C.	55.

| A. 55. | B. 111. | C. 60. |
| A. 56. | B. 31, 32 (cf. 21ª). | C. 67. |

The De Lapidibus of A may probably have been a tract on the Twelve Stones of the Apocalypse.

A. 57.	B. 136.	C. 59.
A. 58.	B. 120.	C. 52.
A. 59.	B. 132.	C. 56.
A. 60.	B. vac.	C. 62.

P. Apollonius is usually called Collatio or Collatino. Poems of his (Hierosolyma, Fasti, etc.) were printed in cent. xv.

A. 61.	B. 107.	C. 54.
A. 62.	B. vac.	C. 57.
A. 63.	B. vac.	C. vac.
A. 64.	B. 123.	C. 61.

Isolae should be Isotae, = Isotta Nogarola (1420–1466): her letters are not printed. Perleone was of Rimini.

A. 65.	B. 128ª	C. 58.
A. 66.	B. 156.	C. 85.
A. 67.	B. 158.	C. vac. ?
A. 68.	B. 157.	C. 83.
A. 69.	B. vac.	C. 84.
A. 70.	B. vac.	C. 82.
A. 71.	B. vac.	C. 86.
A. 72, 73.	B. vac.	C. 87, 88.
A. 74.	B. 161.	C. 71 (or 73).
A. 75, 76.	B. vac.	C. 73 or 74, 75.
A. 77.	B. vac.	C. 76 ?
A. 78.	B. vac.	C. 77.
A. 79.	B. 165.	C. 81.
A. 80.	B. vac.	C. 79 ?
A. 81.	B. 44.	C. 139.
A. 82.	B. vac.	C. 78 ?
A. 83.	B. vac.	C. vac.
A. 84.	B. vac.	C. 80.
A. 85.	B. 10–27, 30, ?31.	C. 181–200.
A. 86.	B. 29 ?	C. 174.
A. 87, 88.	B. vac.	C. 175, 176.
A. 89.	B. 9.	C. 179.
A. 90, 91.	B. 1, 2.	C. 177, 178.
A. 92.	B. 28.	C. 180.
A. 93.	B. 51.	C. 41.
A. 94.	B. 55.	C. 90.
A. 95.	B. 49.	C. 91.
A. 96.	B. 42.	C. 92.
A. 97.	B. 64.	C. 101.
A. 98.	B. vac.	C. 103.
A. 99.	B. 69.	C. 104.
A. 100.	B. 50.	C. 105.
A. 101.	B. 47.	C. 106.

A. 102.	B. 46.	C. 107.
A. 103.	B. 38.	C. 109.
A. 104.	B. vac.	C. 108 ?
A. 105.	B. 48.	C. 102.
A. 106.	B. 37.	C. 93.
A. 107.	B. 53.	C. 94.
A. 108.	B. 54.	C. 95.
A. 109.	B. 39.	C. 96.
A. 110.	B. 45.	C. 100.
A. 111.	B. 43.	C. 99.
A. 112.	B. vac.	C. 123.
A. 113.	B. vac.	C. 98.
A. 114.	B. vac.	C. 126, 127.
A. 115, 116.	B. 62.	C. 125.

The treatise of Neckam de Naturis Rerum ends with a comment on Ecclesiastes.

A. 117.	B. 35.	C. 124.
A. 118.	B. 63.	C. 97.
A. 119.	B. 58.	C. 122.
A. 120.	B. 59.	C. 121.
A. 121.	B. 66.	C. 120.
A. 122.	B. vac.	C. 112.
A. 123.	B. 56.	C. 113.
A. 124.	B. 87.	C. 117.
A. 124.	B. vac.	C. 119 ?
A. 126.	B. vac.	C. 111.
A. 127.	B. vac.	C. 118.
A. 128.	B. 119.	C. vac.

Is the author Cardinal Giovanni di Domenico (d. 1419)?

A. 129.	B. 68.	C. 114.
A. 130.	B. '169.	C. 116.
A. 131.	B. 117.	C. 146.
A. 132.	B. 85.	C. 128.
A. 133.	B. 57 ?	C. 144 (cf. 129).
A. 134.	B. 70.	C. 130.
A. 135.	B. 52.	C. 132.
A. 136.	B. 34.	C. 133.
A. 137.	B. 61.	C. 142.
A. 138.	B. 72.	C. 143.

Probably the poem is Hampole's Prick of Conscience.

A. 139.	B. 91.	C. 145.
A. 140.	B. 65.	C. 131.
A. 141.	B. 170.	C. 141.
A. 142.	B. 36.	C. 136.
A. 143.	B. 164.	C. 137.
A. 144.	B. 71.	C. 135.
A. 145.	B. 153.	C. 134.
A. 146.	B. 88.	C. 140.
A. 147.	B. vac.	C. 115.
A. 148.	B. vac.	C. 138.

A.	149.	B.	75.	C.	150.
A.	150.	B.	40.	C.	147.
A.	151.	B.	76^a.	C.	153?
A.	152.	B.	vac.?	C.	vac.?
A.	153.	B.	76?	C.	154?
A.	154.	B.	147.	C.	149.
A.	155.	B.	vac.	C.	168.
A.	156.	B.	82.	C.	152.
A.	157.	B.	78.	C.	155?
A.	158.	B.	vac.	C.	vac.
A.	159.	B.	83.	C.	156.
A.	160.	B.	77.	C.	157.
A.	161.	B.	vac.?	C.	158?
A.	162.	B.	vac.	C.	159.
A.	163.	B.	79.	C.	160.
A.	164.	B.	80.	C.	161.
A.	165.	B.	93.	C.	163.
A.	166.	B.	94.	C.	164?
A.	167.	B.	78^a?	C.	167?
A.	168.	B.	(cf. 79 last part).	C.	165?
A.	169.	B.	152.	C.	170.
A.	170.	B.	149.	C.	171.
A.	171.	B.	150.	C.	vac.
A.	172.	B.	148.	C.	169.

A.	173.	B.	177.	C.	vac.	Otho C.	xv.
A.	174.	B.	vac.	C.	vac.	Otho C.	xiii.
A.	175.	B.	178.	C.	vac.	Otho C.	xvi.
A.	176.	B.	81.	C.	172.		
A.	177.	B.	89.	C.	173.		
A.	178.	B.	176.	C.	vac. (cf. 217).	Otho D.	xi.
A.	179.	B.	cf. 176^b.	C.	vac.		
A.	180.	B.	60^a, 60^b.	C.	vac.	Otho C.	xiv.
A.	181.	B.	175 (cf. 60^{a-d}: 176^c).	C.	vac.	Otho D.	x.
A.	182.	B.	vac.	C.	vac.	Otho C.	xii.

Here A ends: we continue with B and C.

B.	3, 4.	C.	vac.
B.	5.	C.	vac.
B.	8.	C.	vac.
B.	21.	C.	vac.
B.	41.	C.	vac.
B.	60^d	C.	203.
B.	67.	C.	151?
B.	73.	C.	206.
B.	74.	C.	vac.
B.	84.	C.	vac.
B.	86.	C.	vac.
B.	90.	C.	166?
B.	92.	C.	21.

	B. 114.	C. 24.
	B. 116.	C. 25.
	B. 118.	C. 211.
	B. 121.	C. vac.
A. vac.	B. 122.	C. vac.
(cf. A. 15).	B. 125.	C. vac.
	B. 133.	C. vac.
	B. 137.	C. vac.
	B. 151.	C. vac.
	B. 154.	C. 72.
	B. 155.	C. vac.
	B. 160.	C. vac.
	B. 162.	C. 225.
	B. 163.	C. (cf. 151).
	B. 166.	C. (cf. 213).
	B. 167.	C. (cf. 213).
	B. 168.	C. vac.
	B. 171.	C. 210.
	B. 172.	C. vac.
	B. 173.	C. vac.
	B. 174.	C. vac.

Here B ends.

A. vac.	B. vac.	C. 39.
		C. 40.
A. cf. 51.	B. 104.	C. 49.
		C. 63 still extant.
		C. 69.
A. vac.	B. vac.	C. 70.
		C. 89.
cf. A. 104.		C. 108.
		C. 110.
		C. 148.

This entry gives the monastic provenance (Bury St Edmunds), not the title.

C. 201.
C. 202.
C. 204.
C. 205.
C. 207.
C. 208.
C. 209.
C. 212–230.

These with two doubtful exceptions are wanting in A, B and are clearly for the most part late books.

IV.

THE MANUSCRIPTS NOW PRESERVED IN THE CHAPTER LIBRARY OF WESTMINSTER ABBEY.

In this section of our work a description is given of the manuscripts now in possession of the Dean and Chapter of Westminster, beginning with those kept in the Library. Besides those described in detail there are some volumes and fragments of comparatively recent date, of which no account is given here: for example, three volumes of sermons by Dr Only (1725), a mass of papers by Herbert Thorndike (not, apparently, including any of his work upon Origen), a theological treatise or treatises by Dr Anthony Horneck, and a modern transcript of some of Atterbury's letters. Among manuscripts not kept in the Library, the Islip roll, recently returned to the Abbey by the Society of Antiquaries, seems to need no description. We could add nothing to what is given in the splendid publication by Mr W St John Hope in *Vetusta Monumenta*, issued in 1906.

Our acknowledgments are due to the Rev. R. H. Malden, M.A., King's College, Cambridge, now Classical Lecturer at Selwyn College, who made notes and transcripts from the manuscripts, upon which the descriptions are to some extent based.

1. PENTATEUCHUS HEBRAICE.

Vellum, $6\frac{1}{4} \times 4$, ff. 398, 18 lines to a page. Cent. xiii, very well written.

Stamped leather binding of cent. xvi: clasps gone.

Collation: 1 paper slip. 1^8–22^8 23^6 24^8–27^8 28^6 29^8–40^8 41^4 42^8–50^8 51^2 52^2. 1 paper slip.

At the beginning (xvi):

Liber R. Bruarni.

Liber Ecclesiae Christi Oxon. ex dono Ric. Bruarni A° 1565 Jan. 14.

Of cent. xiv : In isto volumine continentur quinque libri Moysi s. Gen. Ex. Leu. Num. Deut.

Iohannes de Grandissono.

(This is the Bishop of Exeter 1328–1370.)

Primum uolumen Pentatheucum id est v libri Moysi precii iii florenorum.

Contents:

> The Pentateuch in Hebrew, well written, with vowel-points.
> Headlines in Latin in a hand of cent. xiii.
> The book much resembles Dr Caius's Hebrew Bible at Gonville and Caius College, MS. no. 404.
> At the end is an extract of 11 lines from Jerome ad Rusticum, of cent. xiii.
> dum essem iuuenis et in solitudinis
> —dulces fructus capio.

Bruarne was Hebrew Professor at Oxford, Canon of Christ Church and Windsor, and elected Provost of Eton in 1561 but soon after ejected. He died in April 1565 and is buried at Windsor.

I do not know of any evidence besides that afforded by this book that Bp Grandison was a Hebrew scholar.

2.   PSALTERIUM HEBRAICO-LATINUM.

Vellum, $14\frac{7}{8} \times 11\frac{3}{4}$, ff. $38+1$, four columns to a page, of 54 lines. Cent. xiii, finely written.   2 fo. inimicum.

Collation: 1^6 2^8–5^8. 1 paper flyleaf.

The Psalter in Latin (Gallican version) and Hebrew.

The arrangement of the columns is

  1. Lat.   2, 3. Heb.   4. Lat.

The catchwords of the quires are in Hebrew, which indicates that the Hebrew was written before the Latin.

There are hardly any marginal notes, and I detect no marks of ownership.

Similar MSS. are at Trinity College, Cambridge (R. 8. 6), Corpus Christi College, Oxford, and elsewhere: there is on the whole a presumption that they are of Franciscan origin.

3.   BIBLIA. N. 5. 179. (Also G. 212.)

Vellum, $6\frac{1}{8} \times 4\frac{1}{2}$, ff. 492, double columns of 49 lines. Cent. xiii, very good hand.

Old binding.

Collation: 1^4 2^6 | 3^{16}–15^{16} 16^{12} 17^{18} 18^{16} 19^{16} (wants 14) 20^{16}–28^{16} 29^{14} 30^{12} 31^{12} 32^{22} 33^{12} (wants 10–12).

On the flyleaf:

Possidet...
Non licet violare quenquam (?) sui commodi gratia.
N. inquit.

The name Thomas Seale occurs twice, once with the date 1609.

Contents:

> Jerome to Paulinus. Frater Ambrosius.
> Prol. to Pentateuch. Desiderii mei.
> Genesis—2 Chron. Prol. to 2 Chr. Eusebius Ieronimus. Prayer of
>   Manasses follows without break.
> Ezra, Neh., 1 Esdr. (Et fecit), Tobit, Judith, Esther, Job.
> Psalter (Gallican) with a small lacuna : a list of the *Cantica* in red at
>   the end.
> Prov.—Ecclus.
> Isa.—Malachi.
> 1, 2 Macc.
> Evv. Paul. Act. Cath. Apoc.
> Prol. to 2 Macc. Secundus liber hystorie maccabeorum.
> Prol. to Matt. Matheus cum primo.
> Table of books and chapters.
> Verses on the Canon of the Gospels
>   quattuor est primus primis tribus alter opimus
>   ...
>   agnos committit in se librum Ioha finit.
> Table of Lections: called Annotaciones. The Sanctoral seems undistinctive.
> List of the Judges : a short list of church writers, Origen to Alcuin.
> Prophecies of the life of Christ.
> Interpretationes Nominum, Aaz—Zuzim, in triple columns.

Initials:

> *Prol.* a man writing. 2nd *Prol.* similar. *Gen.* decorative.
> 1 *Reg.* man offers lamb. 2 *Reg.* Saul pierces himself.
> *Neh.* man by city on *L.* 1 *Esdr.* man sprinkles altar.
> *Beatus vir.* David plays harp. *Prov.* Solomon chastises Rehoboam.
> *Zech.* single figure. *Matt.* at desk. *Rom.* Paul with sword.

4.   BIBLIA.

Uterine vellum, 6×4, ff. 631, double columns of 42 lines. Cent.
xiii–xiv in a very pretty hand.

Collation: 1^{24}–11^{24} 12^{22} 13^{24} (one slip) 14^{22} 15^{24}–22^{24} 23^{26} 24^{24}–26^{24}
27^{8}.

Contents:

> Proll.
> Gen.—2 Chron. Prayer of Manasses with title in margin.
> Esdr. Neh. 2 Esdr. (Et fecit) Esdr. iii (=4 Esdr.) in 29 chapters.
> Tobit—Job.
> Psalter (Gallican).
> Prov.—Ecclus.
> Isa.—Mal.
> 1, 2 Macc. Proll. of Rabanus.
> Evv. Paul. Act. Cath. Apoc.

Ep. to Laodiceans in later hand.
Interpretationes Nominum. Aaz—Zuzim.

Initials:

   Gen. Six days of Creation, Sabbath, and Crucifixion.
   In the margin of Exod. xxvi. are drawings of the Ark, Candlestick, and Altar
   of Incense, in rather delicate outline.

5.   BIBLIA. G. 210.

Vellum, $6\frac{3}{4} \times 4\frac{1}{2}$, ff. 517, double columns of 49 lines. Cent. xiv?
Collation: 1^4 (blank) 2^{24}–10^{24} 11^{10} (one slip) 12^{24} 13^{24} 14^{22} 15^{24}–21^{24}
22^{28} 23^{24} (one slip) 24^6 (blank: wants one).

Contents:

   Proll.
   Gen.—2 Chron. (Prol. to 2 Chr. Eusebius Ieronimus): Prayer of Manasses.
   Esdr. Neh. 1 Esdr. (et fecit) Tobit—Job.
   Psalter (Gallican).
   Prov.—Ecclus.
   Isa.—Mal.
   1, 2 Macc. Proll. of Rabanus.
   Evv. Paul. Act. Cath. Apoc.
   Interpretationes nominum. Aaz—Zuzim.
   Hebrew alphabet.
   An erased inscription on last leaf of text.
   Printed Kalendar and Almanac (1578–1603).

On the flyleaf are some notes and verses. On the verso a page of
writing erased.

The initials are decorative, in bright colours, and rather effective.

6.   XII PROPHETAE GLOSATI.

Vellum, $11\frac{1}{8} \times 5\frac{5}{8}$, ff. 155, text 14 lines to a page. Cent. xiii, very
well written, good binding of cent. xvi, with two clasps.
Collation: 1^{12}–13^{12} (wants 12).

On the flyleaf at the end are sketches of heads and a lion rampant.
Also some pencil notes, and on the last page at lower right-hand corner
is a large gothic G.

Contents:

   1. Duodecim prophetae glosati . . .   .   . . f. 1
      Prol. of Jerome. Non idem est ordo.
      Gloss begins: Verbum quod a principio.
      Ends: eos qui faciunt opera terrena.

2. Sermon on St Thomas (22 ll. another hand, xiii) . . 151*b*
   Affer manum tuam.
3. Rules for the behaviour of schoolboys (a third hand, xiii):
   printed below 152*b*
4. Note on the man with the withered hand (xiii).
   [2, 3 and 4 are in different hands, but all apparently of the
   xiiith cent.]

Rules for the behaviour of schoolboys.

Quoniam per omnia decet pueros scolari discipline deditos esse facetos ac omni morum honestate pollentes, dignum est ut ad eorum informationem eis aliqua proponantur.

Mane ergo surgentes pueri signent se signo crucis sancte, et dicat unusquisque simbolum, scilicet Credo in deum etc., et ter dominicam orationem, et quinquies salutationem beate virginis, absque clamore et tumultu : quod qui neglexerit bonam subeat disciplinam.

Deinde, lectuli<s> suis tapetis sive suis coopertoriis decenter per omnia coopertis, cameram suam simpliciter sine strepitu simul exeant, et modeste ac lotis manibus ecclesiam adeant, non currendo, neque saltando, nec ecciam garriendo, sed nec alicui inmundo homini vel animali aliquam molestiam inferendo ; non arcum, non baculum, non lapillum in manu gestando, nec aliquid aliud tangendo per quod possit cuiquam noceri ; sed simpliciter et honeste et gradu conposito incedentes.

Intrantes itaque ecclesiam signent se signo crucis, et dicta oratione dominica et salutatione beate virginis cum genuflexione coram crucifixo, surgant et chorum intrent bini et bini humiliter et devote ; et in medio chori inclinantes se modeste versus altare, ad stallum suum sive sedem suam redeat unusquisque : quod qui contempserit disciplinam asperam non euadat.

In choro quidem stantes vel sedentes non habeant occulos deflexos ad laycos, sed pocius versus altare; non ridentes, non garrientes, non cachinnantes, non deridentes alicui si minus bene legit vel psallit; non se mutuo clam vel palam percutientes, neque aspere respondentes cum a casu per majores super aliquo fuerint requisiti : predictorum vero transgressores ictum ferule sentiant sine mora.

Cum vero pueri majores in choro stantes viderint vel sedentes, et ipsi stent vel sedeant, in omnibus et per omnia bonos mores eorum et gestus pro viribus imitantes. Lecturi siquidem, priusquam ascendant ad legendum, in medio chori versus altare humiliter se inclinent, et similiter faciant postquam legerint ad loca sua reuertentes. Dictam vero inclinationem obseruent sive in stallo suo, sive ante gradum presbyterii, cum aliquid ibidem fuerint cantaturi : quod qui non fecerit ictum ferule festinum incurrat.

Chorum quidem nullus hinc inde transeat sine deuota capitis inclinatione versus altare, nec ecciam fiat transitus absque causa evidenti ; circuentes vero altare simili modo gerant eundo et redeundo : alioquin ictum ferule sustinebunt.

Exeuntes quidem eorum (eundem) modum et gestum observare studeant quem intrantes : et similiter domi ab ecclesia vel scola redeuntes sic se habeant, ut superius dictum est : et eandem penam in hac parte sustineant transgressores.

Item, quicunque cum socio, vel cum clerico aliquo, anglice vel gallice latinum intelligens loqui presumpserit, pro quolibet verbo ictum ferule sustineat.

Item, pro qualibet rusticitate dicti vel facti, et pro quolibet iuramento, ferule non parcatur ; set liceat sic jurare : certe, vero, forte, dico vobis, proculdubio, sciat deus. Pro quolibet autem mendacio quilibet subeat disciplinam.

Item, in cujuscunque manu inventi fuerint decii (=dice), pro quolibet puncto ictum virge sentiat super nudum.

Item, quicunque diebus festivis per villam vel per domos rusticorum discurrerit, vel absque certa causa et honesta et majorum licencia extra curiam, vel certum locum ad ludendum moderate prius pueris assignatum, inventus fuerit, bonam in crastino sub[b]eat disciplinam.

Simili modo puniatur qui exierit ab aula diebus predictis antequam magne gratie post prandium domini (? domino) compleantur. In mensa siquidem puerorum qualibet septimana eorum per ordinem presit unus, qui modo communi, quasi ebdomadarius, eis apposita et apponenda benedicat, et refectione completa deo gratias de universis beneficiis debitas referat ac deuotas, et pro viuis ac defunctis suis benefactoribus intercedat.

Item, quicunque hora cubandi lectum sociorum fregerit, vel pannas absconderit, aut calciamenta seu puluinaria de angulo in angulum jactauerit, vel rabiem fecerit, seu familiam turbauerit, duram in crastino subeat disciplinam.

Euntes autem cubitum sic se habeant ut surgentes, signantes se et suos lectulos signo crucis.

7.   EPISTOLAE PAULI CUM COMMENTO.

Vellum, $11\frac{7}{8} \times 7\frac{7}{8}$, ff. 147, double column of 50 lines.   Cent. xii–xiii, in a fine round hand.

Binding of cent. xvi : metal loop above lower clasp on first cover.

At the end (xvi) :

Liber monasterii de Chertesey.

2 fo. euangelii.

Collation : 1⁴ (blank : wants one : one paper slip) 2⁸–17⁸ 18¹² 19⁴ (blank : wants one : one paper slip).

Contents :

The Pauline Epistles with comment.   The text is written in red.

Inc. A ciuitate metropoli achaie regionis grecorum scripsit apostolus paulus romanis hanc epistolam quos non ipse non petrus non quilibet discipulorum xii^cim primum instruxit.

1 Cor.   Precepto domini saluatoris admonitus ap. paulus uenit Corinthum.

2 Cor.   Apostolo recedente a chorinthiis.

1 Thess. Macedonia prouincia est grecorum.

2 Thess. Thessalonicenses accipientes priorem epistolam.

1 Tim.   Timotheus filius fuit mulieris iudee.

2 Tim.   Secundam epistolam timotheo scripsit ab urbe.

Gal.   Primo querendum est in exordio huius ep. unde appellati sint galathe.

Eph.   Ephesus ciuitas est asye et grecie.

Col.   Colosenses sunt asiani.   This has a very gay initial.

Phil.   Philipenses sunt macedones .i. greci.

Heb.   In primordiis huius ep. dicendum est.

Philem. Beato apostolo predicatione euangelica intonante in asia.

Tit. Transiens apostolus a creta insula ad alias nationes.

—quorum fides perfectissima erat. *gratia et pax a deo patre nostro et I. C. saluatore nostro.* In margin, contemporary: ℞ deficit.

8.   NEW TESTAMENT IN ENGLISH. N. 5. 178.

Vellum, $4\frac{1}{2} \times 3\frac{3}{8}$, ff. 389, double columns of 27 lines. Cent. xv, in a clear rather rough hand.

Collation: $1^4\ 2^8\ 3^6$ (wants one blank) 4^8–$49^8\ 50^4$.

On flyleaf:

Donum ducissae Richmondiae Henrico com: Arundell. Modo Ric. Wiclife ex dono ipsius prenobilis comitis mens. Sept. 1576.

Contents:

The New Testament in English.

Preceded by a Table of Epistles and Gospels for the Year.

Here biginniþ þe newe testament. prologus of Mᵗ

    Matheu þᵗ was of iude.

At the bottom of the page (xvi): Arundel.

Evv. Paul. Act. Cath. Apoc. with prologues.

Forshall and Madden (I. xlv.) identify this with no. 85 or 86 of the list of MSS. in Bernard's *Catalogi.* They assign the date as about 1450. The version is the later Wycliffite.

9.   PSALTER.

Vellum, $8 \times 5\frac{3}{8}$, ff. 142, 22 lines to a page. Cent. xv, probably written in Flanders for English use. There are fairly good borders and initials but no figures.

Collation: 1^{12}–$11^{12}\ 12^8\ 13^2$.

On flyleaf:

J. Essen [in faded ink, and below it] D. D. Jni. Bayres 1802.

Contents:

Kalendar.

Psalter with Canticles, Quicunque vult and Litany.

Office of the Dead.

In a later hand on the last page is a prayer of Erasmus, printed below.

The Kalendar is Sarum.

Feb. At Feb. 11 in margin partly cut (N)atiuitas Edwardi / filii Mauricii / Berkeley militis / aᵒ dⁿⁱ millesimo / ccccxxxiᵒ et aᵒ / henrici sexti xᵒ / apud Bisterne /.

Mar. David. Cedde.

July. Anne in red.

Aug. Ruthburge (*sic*).
Sept. Edithe, red.
Oct. Wlfranni, red.
Frediswide, red.
Nov. Wynefride, red.
Dep. S. Edmundi C, red.
Hugonis, red.
Dec. Osmundi, red.

In the Litany:

Apostles. Marcialis. *Martyrs.* Eustachi cum soc., Nichasi c. s., Luciane c. s., Corneli, Cipriane, Leonides over erasure. These end the list. There are few Confessors. *Virgins* end with : Fides, Spes, Caritas, Iuliana.

At the end:
Pie precationes per Eras. Rot. conscripte.

Accedentis ad sacram Synaxim.

Ago tibi gratias, Jesu Christe, pro ineffabili charitate, quod genus humanum tua morte redimere dignatus es, et oro ne patiaris tuum sacrosanctum sanguinem pro me frustra fusum esse, sed tuo corpore semper pascas animum meum, ut paulatim adolescens virtutum auctibus, efficiar idoneum membrum corporis tui mystici, quod est Ecclesia, nec unquam deficiam ab illo sanctissimo foedere, quod in extrema coena distributo pane et porrecto poculo pepigisti cum discipulis tuis electis, et per hos cum omnibus qui per baptismum in societatem tuam insiti sunt. Amen.

10. MANUALE.

Vellum, 8½ × 7, ff. 12, 24 lines to a page. Cent. xv, in fine upright English hand. Music on four-line stave.

Fragment of a manual, formerly used as covers to Dering's music-books.

Containing:

Ordo ad facienda sponsalia . . . . f. 1
The formulae are in English : of the Use of York. There is a gap after f. 4 which has carried away the Sequence.
Causa autem quare sunt vii^tem sacramenta 7
Ordo uisitandi infirmi 7b
defectione :
The fragment ends with part of the office of the dead.
The first quire is now of 8 leaves : a gap after f. 4.
The second quire has 4 leaves remaining.

11. GENEALOGIAE BIBLIAE ETC.

Vellum, 5 × 3½, ff. 4 + 44 + 4, text in double columns of 34 lines. Cent. xiii, late, well written.

Collation: a⁴ 1⁸(?) 2 (eight) 3 (five) 4²⁴ (wants 24) 5⁴.

Part of f. 1 with beginning of text is cut out.

Diagram of the twelve tribes : in a circle . . . . . f. 2

On 2b, 3, diagrams in frames formed like church-windows of *a* Judges, *b* Stations in the wilderness.

On 3b diagram of the tribes in the Promised Land, circular.

The Biblical genealogies are continued (irregularly) on the *L.* page. The text, with accounts of the persons mentioned, is on the *R.* or on both.

The continuous text ends with Tiberius : the genealogies with the Apostles and Barnabas.

On a subsequent page is a table of the Holy Family. After six blank pages are accounts of Philip, James, the destruction of Jerusalem, and John Evangelist.

On 44b are late scribbles.

12. LEGENDA AUREA.

Vellum, 11½ × 8, ff. 308, double columns of 39 lines. Cent. xiv, in good English hand.

Old binding, red skin over boards : clasps gone : a metal loop for chaining just above the lower clasp on the first cover. On the back is the mark D iȜ.

The same is on the leaf after the Kalendar, erased : D iȜ continet legendum sanctorum. Erasure below.

Collation: 1⁸ 2¹²–26¹².

Contents :

1. Kalendar . . . . f. 2
2. Jac. de Voragine Legenda Aurea 8
   Prol. Universum tempore.
   Tabula : divided into Tempus renouationis, reconciliationis, deuiationis, reconciliationis, peregrinationis.
   Text. Aduentus domini per iiij septimanas.
3. Hugo Cardinalis de confessione 304b
   Confessio debet esse preuisa amara uerecunda discreta
   —sal terre orbis lumen sacerdotem altissimi vicarium Christi.
   Finito libro reddamus gloriam Christo. Deo gratias.
4. Extracts. *a.* Jerome to Asella. Antequam domum sancte paule uorsem.
   b. Jerome to Augustine.
   c. Verses.

In the Kalendar :

Notes of diet and beverage for the several months are added at the bottom of the pages.

Feb. has original note : Hec sunt festa ix lectionum in quibus non habetur expositio euangelii ad matutinas.

Mar. 22 added : a.d. m.ccc^{mo} vicesimo primo.　Decapitatus fuit thomas comes
　　　　lancastr. apud pontefractum.　Erasure follows.
　　　　Cedde is entered, not David.
Ap. 29.　Peter Martyr added.
Sept. 5.　Bertin added.
　　　　Edith and Firmin added.
Note :　Mem. quod a.d. m.ccc^{mo} vicesimo sexto in festo S. Michaelis archang.
　　　　domina regina anglie rediit in angliam.　Et sic erat pax reformata
　　　　inter d. regem Edwardum anglie et d^{nam} reginam uxorem suam.
In pencil : Fest. S. Sabine et sauin(i)ane et sauine iiii^{to} die.
Oct. 2 added.　Transl. S. Thome herefordensis.　ix lect. omnino feriand.
　　　　6.　Transl. S. Hugonis.
　　　　Wlfrani, fridesuuide, neoti.
Dec. 8.　Concept. b. M. v. added.

The following legends are inserted in the text :

After Matthias　　　　　　xlv　　Cedda.
　　　Benedict　　　　　　xlviii　Cuthbert.
　　　Pancras　　　　　　lxxi　　Dunstan.
　　　Petronilla　　　　　lxxiii　Augustine.
　　　vii fratres　　　　　lxxxvi Mildride, Kenelm.
　　　Nazarius and Celsus xcvii　Sampson.
　　　Savinian and Savina cxxiii Sabina.
　　　Brice　　　　　　　clxii　Edmund C., Hugo, Edmund R.

Text ends with Pelagius and dedicatio Ecclesie.

13.　　　　　GRAYSTON SUPER SENTENTIAS.

Vellum, 14¼ × 9⅝, ff. 306, double columns of 64 lines.　Cent. xv.
Old binding, skin over boards, clasps gone : metal loop above lower
clasp on first cover : another formerly at bottom of first cover.

　　　　　　　　　　　　　　　　　　　　2 fo. firme.

Collation : 1^{12}–5^{12} (wants 7–12) 6^{12}–17^{12} 18^4 19^{12}–23^{12} 24^{10} 25^{12}–27^{12}
28^4 (wants 2–4).

Contents :

　1.　Doctor Grayston monachus Dunelmensis super Sentencias　f.　1
　　　　Dirupit petram et fluxerunt aque
　　　　qui possunt habere actum intendendi diuersum.
　2.　Eiusdem (?) quaestiones.
　　　　Utrum ex principiis (?) creditis possit haberi sciencia
　　　　proprie dicta　.　　.　　.　　.　　.　　.　　.　　55
　　　　—secundum eos oritur et inter[er]it quicquid oritur.

I have not hitherto been able to detect another copy of this work.

14.   GERVASE OF CHICHESTER.

Paper, 11½ × 7¼, ff. 127, 30 lines to a page.   Cent. xvi, well written.
Collation: one slip, 1⁸–16⁸ (wants 8).

At beginning and end are fragments of service-books of cent. xiv and xv.

At the beginning is:

> Liber Nicho. Hickett subde(cani) 29° Julij 1562.

1. Gervasius presbiter Cicestrensis super Malachiam prophetam
   de ordinis sacerdotalis instructione .   .   .   .   . f. 1
       In 13 books : beginning in lib. IV.
   positus ubi caput membrorum potius nutu deflectitur
       —Saluatore nostro J. C. qui cum Patre et Sp. S. viuit
       et regnat et gloriatus deus per immortalia sec. sec.
       Amen.
2. Sermo eiusdem in festo S. Thome Cant. 119*b*
   Preached at Chichester in the first year of the author's
   ordination.
   Quis est hic et laudabimus eum ? Fecit enim mirabilia in
   vita sua
       —et placabilem fraterni sceleris vindictam exercuit.

This MS. is mentioned by Tanner as being a transcript of the Royal MS. 3. B. X.

15.   MARTIALIS.

Vellum, 10½ × 7, ff. 57, double columns of 50 lines.   Cent. xiii and xiv ?   Written in England.
Collation: 1⁸–4⁸ (wants 1) 5¹⁰ 6⁸ 7⁸.

Either this or no. 16 was given by Dr Robert Freind.   See Register.

1. Martialis Epigrammata.
   Wanting VIII. xxxviii. l. 5 to lxii. l. 4.
         X. xiv. l. 5 to XII. xci. l. 3.
2. Epigrammata Godfredi Wintoniensis Abbatis monasterii Sancti Swithuni
   qui floruit sub Henrico primo.   Ob. 1107.
   This title in Dean Goodwin's (?) hand.
   Edited by T. Wright, *Satirical Poets of the Twelfth Century*, Rolls Series, II.
   p. 103.
   Inc : Undique susceptum qui miscuit utile dulci.   Wright, p. 103.
   Ends : ditior ecce fuit (l.c. p. 146).
3. Martialis liber de spectaculis.
   The last four epigrams absent.
4. Versus Sidonii (Ausonii) de xii imperatoribus
       Cesareos proceres
           —sed iusta piacula fratrem.
5. Tractatus de simbolo.
       Christiane religionis summa
           —operam impendere sed memorie.
   On p. 1 the name Wylton.

16. MARTIALIS EPIGRAMMATA.

Paper, $8\frac{3}{8} \times 5\frac{5}{8}$, ff. 209, 27–28 lines to a page. Cent. xv, written in Italy.

Collation: 1^6 2^8–4^8 5^{10}–14^{10} 15^8 16^{12} 17^8 18^{12} 19^8 20^{12} 21^8 22^{12} (wants 12).

Initials scarlet and blue alternately. Titles of epigrams in red. Initial B at the beginning in red leaving a branch-pattern in white.

Contents:

Martialis Epigrammatum libri.
In lib. 1, Epigrams 17–41 (ad Avitum to ad Lividum) follow 104 (ad Scaevolam).
27 ad Sextilianum is here 92.
33 ad Sabidium 98.
34 de Gellia 99.
63 de Laevina 40.
On f. 1 is a mutilated inscription,
Matthaeus Cotton jure me vindicat.
The writer of this adds a metrical translation of four epigrams in Lib. I, signing them 'Cotton,' or 'per Cotton,' and also supplies, on the margin of the last remaining leaf, the last seven of the Apophoreta which have perished with the last leaf.
The last four epigrams of the de Spectaculis are absent.

17. ARATOR, ETC. Press-mark N. 5. 183.

Vellum, $8\frac{5}{8} \times 6$, ff. 57, 28 and 24 lines to a page. Cent. xi–xii, in a hand resembling that of Christ Church, Canterbury.

2 fo. reprimit.

Collation: 1^4 2^8–6^8 7^{10} | 8^4 (wants 3).

From the Franciscan convent at Lincoln: on the flyleaf is:

·2╫ In isto uolumine continentur actus apostolorum uersificati et est de communitate fratrum minorum Lincoln. 20. 31. 25.

There is also the beginning of a letter of xvith cent. in English: no names are mentioned.

Contents:

1. A short tract without title, mainly on the Virtues.
   Philosophia est inquisitio rerum humanarum . . f. 1
   Ending f. 3: laus apud deum.
2. Aratoris Subdiaconi Historia Apostolica 3*b*
   Domino Sancto...Floriano Abbati Arator...
   Qui meriti florem
   —quod pia causa iuuat.

Domino Sancto...Papae Vigilio Arator...
Moenibus undosis
—laus monitoris erit.
Capitula.
Text: Ut sceleris iudea...
Lib. II. f. 26 b: ends at line 1155 lucem factura perennem. Wanting ll. 1156–1250.

There are glosses, decreasing in number towards the end of the poem. The MS. is mentioned by Uffenbach, *Merkwürdige Reisen*, II. 515.

18.　　　　JOSEPHUS ISCANUS. N. 5. 187.

Vellum, $7\frac{5}{8} \times 5$, ff. 49, 39 lines to a page. Cent. xiii, very well written.　　　　　　　　　　　　　　　　　　　2 fo. Thetios.
Collation: 1^2 (1 lines cover) 2^8–7^8.
A note from Bale on the flyleaf.
Also Liber Guilhelmi Camdeni Londin.
Iouis omnia plena.

Contents:

Josephi Iscani (= of Exeter) de bello Troiano libri sex.
Iliadum lacrimas concessaque pergama fatis.
Lib. II. f. 8, III. 15 b, IV. 21 b, v. 28 b, VI. 35 b.
Ending
Quam pascit presens extremaque terminat etas
Frigii daretis yl(i)ados liber sextus expl.

On the margin of f. 48 is written (in Camden's hand?) "Antiocheidos libri," the name of another poem by the same author.

Another MS. of the present poem is Bodl. Digby 157. The Westminster MS. is mentioned by Tanner. The poem was printed at Basel in 1541 and 1585, and elsewhere.

The initial at the beginning is the length of the page, and has a good deal of silver branch-work on gold ground: it is of very good execution.

19.　　　IOH. DE ALTA VILLA ARCHITRENIUS. N. 5. 182.

Vellum, $7\frac{5}{8} \times 5$, ff. 72, 31 lines to a page. Cent. xiv, well written.
　　　　　　　　　　　　　　　　　　　　　　2 fo. Incola.
Collation: 1^8–5^8 6^6 7^{10} 8^8 9^8

Contents:

Iohannis de Alta Villa Architrenius.
Inc. liber Architrenii
 Velificatus athos dubio mare ponte ligato.
Ends : Equet in eternum populi dilectus et ostrum:
   Finem composui da mihi quod merui.

Text edited by T. Wright, *Satirical Poets of the Twelfth Century*,
Rolls Series, Vol. I.
There is a good initial V with gold and silver work at the beginning.

20.   TRACT. DE SPHAERA ETC. N. 5. 188.

Vellum and paper, $6\frac{7}{8} \times 5\frac{1}{8}$, ff. 38, 28 lines to a page. Cent. xiv and
xv, vellum wrapper.
 Collation: 1^8 2^{14} (wants 9, 10, 13, 14) 3^{22} (wants 19–22 : 1, 4, 7, 11,
16 and corresponding leaves vellum, the rest paper).

Contents:

1. Joh. de Sacro Bosco tractatus de spera . . . . f. 1
   Tractatus de spera in quattuor capitula
    ...aut mundana machina dissoluetur.
      Expl. tract. de spera.
  ff. 17, 18a blank.
2. Tract on Arithmetic (xv late) 18*b*
   Quoniam arithmetica circa numerum versetur potis-
    simum
   ...2a species que addicio vocatur.
3. A Christmas Carol in English (xv) 20
   A babe ys borne I wys
   This worlde to ioy & blis
   His ioy shall never fade and misse
   And Ihesus is hys name.

   On cristmasse day at morne
   Thys childe was i borne } & Ihesus.
   To save us alle that were for lorne.

   On gudde friday so sone
   To dethe he was i done } & Ihesus.
   Be twyx all morne and none.

   On Estyr day so swythe
   He rose fro dethe to lyve } & Ihesus.
   To make us all bothe gladde and blythe.

   On the holy Thursday
   To heven he toke hys way } & Ihesus.
   Ther to a byde for euer and day.

4. Astronomical diagram in the hand of no. 1, with text . 20*b*
5. Grammatical tract 21
>   Duo enim sunt oratoris officia si casus exiget aut
>   dilatandi aut breuiandi.
>   There is an illustration in English on f. 36.
>   Ends 37*a*:
>>   lacessiti mesticia suspiriarum cordiatus sarcina fatiga-
>>   mur.
6. Grammatical verses (59) 37*b*
>   ...] precedens mediasque sequencia primo.
>   Ends: Cum tenus absque sine citra circa sunt [....
>   There is a drawing of a female saint (?): upper part of
>   figure only.

On 38*b* are scribbles: the name John Foster occurs: also the date
1489, and a motto on a scroll: audaces fortuna iuuat.

21.   FRENCH POEMS.

Paper, 11⅛ × 8¼, ff. 79, 31 lines to a full page. Cent. xv.
Vellum wrapper: the name Robert Acland is upon it.
Collation: 1⁸ (wants 1: three mutilated) 2¹⁶ (one mut.) 3¹⁴ (wants
three) 4¹⁴ (wants one) 5¹⁶ 6¹² (wants two) 7¹⁰ (fragments).
There are some scribbles in English, Greek and Latin on various
pages. A full account of the contents is given in the *Bulletin de la
Soc. des Anciens Textes Français*, 1875, p. 25.

22.   BESTIARY.

Vellum, 2 × 6¼, ff. 64, 33 lines to a page. Cent. xiii, in a good hand.
Formerly bound with Giraldus Cambrensis (no. 23).
From the Franciscan convent of York (see at end).
Collation: 1¹²–5¹² 6⁴.

Contents:

1. Iste liber uocatur liber Bestiarius.
>   Cum uoluntas conditoris
>>   —erma quippe grece masculus affrodi femina dicitur.
>   Dicuntur in singulis gentibus quedam monstra.
>   Ends with the Panothii
>>   —Reliquas species potest diligens lector prout uoluerit uel tetris
>>   litteris uel aureis luculentius describere (corr. from -itur).
>   On f. 1*b* a full page picture in 3 tiers: the grounds are blue, red,
>   and blue.
>>   *a.* Three figures. *L.* with hand on breast, *C.* points to his
>>   mouth, *R.* has four feet.

b. *L.* has three arms, *C.* has an enormous *R.* hand, *R.* nude, stooping.

c. *L.* Cyclops, *C.* no neck, holds a halbert, *R.* nude, with one breast : holds sword and shears.

On f. 3*a* full page picture : grounds red-brown.

On *L.* a huge man in blue with a triple face points *R.* to a pygmy in close cap with halbert standing in a (conventional) tree.

In front on *C.* a nude *sciapous* in red cap reclines and holds up his enormous foot.

In front on *R.* two men and two women in a cave. These are Bragmanni.

f. 4 has a half-page picture with blue ground. Adam, robed, sits on *L.* naming the beasts assembled on *R.*: a hare or rabbit in front of the rest : the monkey bestrides the deer.

Text. De nominibus animalium   .   .   .   . f. 4
         Omnibus animantibus Adam.

After this some extracts from Bernardus francus (i.e. Bern. Silvester) followed by section beginning
         Bouem greci boeti dicunt.

The pictures represent :

1. Bos, light red.
2. Bugle, dark.
3. La vache et le juenke et le chor.
4. Le motuns et les berbis et le aignel et le pastur. Shepherd on *R.* with crook and horn.
5. Hircus, eating tree.
6. Le porche.
7. Asinus et burdo.
8. Onager.
9. Equus, white.
10. Mulus.
11. Camelus.
12. Dromedarius without hump.
13. Cerf.
14. Dama.
15. Caprea.
16. Aper, attacks dog.
17. Leo retreats on *R.*, hunter blows horn on *L.*
18. Leo cum fetu et leena: roars over dead cub, tree in *C.*
19. Leonis miraculum (recognises a condemned man). Nude man bound to stake in *C.*, lion and spectators on *L.*, others on *R.*
20. Pardus.
21. Lina.
22. Pantera, followed by beasts on *R.*, the dragon puts its tail into its ear.
23. Ursus licking its formless whelp into shape.
24. Rinoceros. Unicorn lays its head in a maiden's lap : the hunter pierces it.
25. Monoceros.
26. Tigris looking at a round mirror while a man on foot steals her cub.
27. Grifes, devours a man.

28. Antalops, horns caught in a bush.
29. Almost full page. Elephas, two-storied castle on his back, full of mailed men.
30. Manticora with a human head.
31. Prandaxum.
32. Eale.
33. Symie ; apes carry off their young in their arms and on their backs when pursued.
34. Castor, pursued, bites off its glands.
35. Lupus, by sheepfold, dog and shepherd asleep.
36. Vulpis, pretends to be dead, a bird explores its mouth.
37. Hyena eating a dead body.
38. Bonacon, pierced by a hunter.
39. Ybex.
40. Canis catches hare.
41. Dog detects a murderer, his master's corpse lies, wounded ; on *R*. a dog takes food to a prisoner in a tower.
42. Dog detects a man stealing an ox.

43. Lepus.	44. Istrix.	45. Cuniculi.	46. Melo.
47. Musio siue murilegus.	48. Mustela.		49. Talpa.
50. Glires, like worms, without legs.		51. Cyrogrillus, squirrel.	

52. Ericius : hedgehogs by apple-trees collect apples on their spines.
53. Amphibia, has devoured a man, his head seen in its mouth (really meant for a crocodile).
54. Luter. The title of the picture is 'vulgo,' the text says Est quedam bestia que vulgo luter dicitur.
55. Formica by corn-field.
56. Apes, flying about a hive on *R.*, man with a white cloth : behind him, man with sickle.
57. Mors, a strange figure like a chrysalis in dark swathings, winged, holding a red triple hook : a man in bed on *R.*

The text of this is called *Mine Mortis* and is a dialogue.

Mine. Egrotas.

Respondetur. Venit tempus quo experimentum mei caperem. Non in mari tantum aut in prelio uir fortis apparet. Exhibetur et lectulo uirtus.

Ending : non sepelliemur sed proiiciemur.

Expl. de bestiis. Inc. de generibus auium . . . . . f. 34
Aves dicte sunt eo quod uias.

The pictures represent :

1. Aquila.	2. Vultur.	3. Grus.	4. Cyconia.
5. Olor.	6. Ardea.	7. Buccon.	8. Ybis.
9. Unnamed : like *ardea*.			

10. Fenix, striped vertically with blue, orange, green, mauve, *R.*, stands on an orange nest, the side of which is hatched with green lines.
11. Caradrius, one at the head of a man in bed, another flying away.
12. Assida or Strabi-(struthio-)camelon, eating stones or eggs.

13. Ericinea.	14. Sulica (Fulica).	15. Alcion.	16. Mergus.
17. Coturnix.	18. Diomedia.	19. Anas.	20. Pitacus (Psitt-).
21. Pelicanus, in its piety.	22. Upupa.	23. Accipiter.	

24. Miluus.	25. Perdix.	26. Pica.	27. Cucus or Cuculus.
28. Coruus.	29. Monedula.	30. Vespertilio.	31. Noctua.
32. Bubo.	33. Lucinia.	34. Turtur.	35. Columba.
36. Hyrundo.	37. Alauda and Merula.		38. Pascer.
39. Turdus.	40. Furfurio.	41. Ficedula and Carduellus.	
42. Pauo, almost full page.	43. Gallus.		

Ends : unde et eoum sidus luciferum dicimus.

Expl. de auibus. Et inc. de piscibus . . . . . f. 42

Pisces dicti unde et pecus a pascendo.

The pictures represent :
1. Balena (walrus-like).
2. Belua, ship about to moor to its back : fishes crowd into its mouth.

3. Delphis.	4. Lupus.	5. Mullus.	6. Mugilis.
7. Gladius.	8. Cesta.	9. Mellanurus..	10. Squatus.
11. Burbulus.	12. Echinus.	13. Allec.	14. Anguilla.
15. Murena.	16. Polipus.	17. Cancrus (a very odd picture).	
18. Conche and Coclee.	19. Ostrea.	20. Musculi.	
21. Peloris.	22. Fungia.	23. Spongia (a sort of worm).	
24. Torpedo (a star-fish).	25. Ulligo.		

Ends (with Ypotamus): et hunc nilus gignit.

Expl. de piscibus. Inc. de serpentibus . . . . f. 46

Anguis generale omnium serpentium nomen est quod complicari
et torqueri potest.

The pictures represent :
1. Anguis, a two-legged dragon.
2. Draco with two legs and two wings.
3. Basiliscus with cock's head.
4. Vipera, the heads of its young project from its sides.
5. Aspic, a man with staff on *R*. (charming it): it puts its tail into its ear.

6. Dipsas.	7. Prester.	8. Ypnalis.	9. Emorois.
10. Serastis, horned.	11. Si talis (Scytalis).	12. Amphisbena.	
13. Boas (sucking a cow).	14. Iaculus.	15. Ydrus.	
16. Celidrus.	17. Rinatrix (Natrix).	18. Sapingua.	
19. Centripeda.	20. Lacertus.	21. Botrax.	22. Sal(a)mandra.
23. Stellio.	24. Snake changing its skin : curious.	25. Vermis.	
26. Aranea.	27. Sanguissuga.	28. Scorpio.	29. Cantanda.
30. Limax.	31. Rana.	32. Three-headed dog, Cerberus.	

33. Chimera : large : with human face, two legs, serpent's tail, ending in
a head.
34. Ypocentaurus.
35. Lapides igniferi, green discs, each containing a human head—male and
female. Orange flames rise from their edges.

Text ends : copiosus ex ambobus ignis consurgit.

2. De rota fortune . . . . f. 54

Naturam diffinire difficile esse asserit tullius....

Fortunam a fortunis nomen habere...

...Item stabilis que manens dat cuncta moueri.

A picture : the wheel of Fortune on blue ground turned by
Fortune who stands behind it. The usual four figures surround

it, and the legend Regnabo. Regno. Regnaui. Sum sine regno. has been scribbled on the tire.

3. De remediis fortuitorum conferunt inter se Callio et Seneca   . 55
G. Dolor imminet. S. Si exiguus est feramus, leuis est patientia.
The latter part deals with women : ends :
pocius quam tuo labore quesita in inrectos usus relinquere.

4. De septem mirabilibus mundi 57
Primum de septem mirabilibus mundi est capitolium rome.
—xx. viii columpnae faciunt finem tam mirabilis edificii.

5. Rubric : Omnia uana esse et res ex fide sua cuique respondere.
Ex poli cancro Iohannis (= Policraticon of John of Salisbury)   58
In creatoris prorumpis iniuriam quicunque ex constellationibus.
—Sic gratiam dei et huius malitie exercitum nemo sequitur.

In red :
Expl. liber de generibus hominum et bestiarum domesticarum, bestiarum ferarum, auium, piscium, draconum et serpentium, omniumque reptilium sine uermium, apium uel muscarium (!) siue monstrinum (!), de morte. Et rota fortune, de diuinationibus sortilegis et nigromanciis et duabus petris. Et de vij miraculis mundi.

On 68 *b*.   A head (xvi?) with flying hair.
An erased name, and date 1555, 12 Augusti, below.

69.   Three distichs of cent. xvi.

69 *b*.   Robert howstayne (xvi).

70.   Notes by him, signed R. h.

70 *b*.   Biga.
Biga communitatis fratrum minorum Ebor. (twice).
Iste liber est de communitate fratrum minorum Ebor.

23.   GIRALDUS CAMBRENSIS. N. 5. 184.

Vellum, 9 × 6, ff. 69, double columns of 28 lines.   Cent. xii–xiii, in a rather large hand.

Formerly bound with the Bestiary (no. 22), of which it has the flyleaf.

Collation : 1¹² (wants one) 2¹²–5¹² 6¹⁰.   2 fo. sicut arma.

At top of p. 1 an old inscription in four words has been cut off : the last word but one was *de*.

Flyleaves :

Bestiarium. 5.
(In i)sto libro continentur
Liber qui vocatur bestiarius.
Item rota fortune.
Item seneca de remediis fortuitorum.

Item prouerbia et historie contra mulieres et uxores.

Item de 7 mirabilibus mundi.

Item excepcio de policraticon iohannis de diuinacionibus sortelegiis nigro-mancia et 2^bus petris.

Contents :

> Giraldi Cambrensis Topographia Hiberniae.
> Prol : Consideranti mihi quam breuis...
> 　　...negocia multa.
> Expl. pref. libri Girardi Camb(r)ensis de mirabilibus hibernie In tres particulas libellus iste distinguitur.
> Capitula (lib. I.).
> 　　Expl. cap. Inc. tropologia de hibernia　.　.　.　. f. 6
> In green : Illustri anglorum regi H. secundo suus Giraldus.
> 　　Placuit excellentie uestre. Red initial.
> Dist. II. f. 22, III. 42 b, ending
> 　　a tanta maiestate fuerit iniunctum.

This copy is noticed in the Rolls edition of Giraldus (v. p. xvi.). It is there said to contain the second edition of the work, and to be very incorrectly written.

24.　　　　　FLORES HISTORIARUM.　151. 7.

Vellum, 12⅜ × 7⅞, ff. 374, double columns of 40 lines.　Cent. xiv, finely written and ornamented.

Binding of cent. xvi.　Clasps gone.

Collation : 1⁸ 2¹² 3¹² 4¹⁰ 5¹² 6¹² 7¹⁰ 8⁴ 9¹⁰ 10¹² 11¹² 12⁸ 13¹² 14¹² 15¹⁰ 16¹²–21¹² 22¹⁰ 23¹²–26¹² 27¹⁰ 28¹²–33¹².

On a label pasted on to p. 1 : Flores Historiarum Matthei Westmonasteriensis Monachi : in a fine xvith cent. hand, perhaps that of John Stow.

Inc. prol. in librum qui (erasure) intitulatur.

> Temporum summam lineam quam descendentem ab exordio.

Ends : scilicet dimidiam partem postulati.

Initials, red and blue alternately.

The following pictures occur :

f.　1.	Man writing at desk.	
83.	Coronation of Arthur by two bishops, blue ground : larger than the rest, a goldfinch at top of the initial.	
167.	Athelstan on his death-bed, minute work.	
168.	Coronation of Eadred, minute work.	
173.	Eadgar on his death-bed, a bishop stands over him, minute work.	
174.	Coronation of Alfred, minute work.	
188.	,,	,, Harold I., minute work.
191.	,,	,, Edward the Confessor, larger.
204.	,,	,, William I., larger.
208.	,,	,, William II., larger.
216.	,,	,, Stephen, brown ground, larger.

220. Coronation of Henry II., brown ground, larger.
227. „ „ Richard I., blue ground, medium size.
232. „ „ John, blue ground, larger.
296. In margin *forma denarii* in red outline.

These pictures are of very fine quality. The best is the coronation of Arthur.

On the last page is an erasure.

The MS. was used for the Rolls edition, see vol. I. p. xix.

The Chetham MS. of the Flores (*ibid.* I. xii.) was formerly the property of the Abbey: see above, p. 25.

25. BRUTE CHRONICLE.

Vellum, $9\frac{1}{8} \times 6\frac{3}{8}$, ff. 98, 29 lines to a page. Cent. xiv, late.
Old binding.
Collation: 1^2 2^8–4^8 (wants 5) 5^8 6^8 7^2 8^8–10^8 11^{10} 12^6 13^{10} 14^2 15^4 (wants one).

Contents:

Chronicle of England in French from Brutus to the execution of Roger Mortimer (1330).
 Ci poet homme sauer coment quant e de quele gent.
—Et apres la Pake le roy fist crier solempne tournement a Derteford . . . . f. 92*b*
Pen-trials of cent. xvi in which the name of Richard Malenger of London occurs.
Table of dates in British history, ranging from 1100 B.C. (foundation of London) to 1382 A.D. (earthquake).

26. CHRONICLE ETC.

Vellum and paper, $7\frac{3}{4} \times 5\frac{1}{2}$, ff. 128, 22 lines to a page. Cent. xiv, in a rather current hand.
Vellum wrapper (fragmentary).
Collation: 1^{12} (wants 1 and 3) 2^{22} 3^{22} (wants 1, 22) 4^{18} (wants two ? 10, 11) 5^{18} 6^{18} 7^{16} 8^{18} (1–9 left).

Contents:

1. Chronicle, beginning imperfectly . . . . . f. 1
 The first complete entry is
  A. d. m° c. apud Westmon. coronacio Henrici fratris Willelmi Rufi qui regnauit xxxvi annis.
 It goes to 1323 : Anno sequenti truncacio domini Andree de Harcla Comitis Carliol.

This portion is connected with the Cistercian Abbey of Newminster in Northumberland.

Quomodo deus flagellauit ducem lancastrie (*l.* austrie) pro capcione Regis Ricardi.
Prima flagellacio. Omnes ciuitates terre illius sunt igne

Quomodo rex Johannes subpeditauit sanctam ecclesiam tempore suo Johannes rex conuocauit omnes abbates

A. d. m⁰. cc⁰. xiii⁰ Johannes Rex Angl. soluens domino pape m^{le} marc. arg. singulis annis fecit homagium in forma

Anglos et leges hic iterando leges.
Reges maiores referam siue nobiliores.
Quanto regnarunt et ubi gens hos tumularunt
Mille quater decabis fit adam bruto prior annis.
Brutus consilio cuiusdam diane classe parata...(4 lines).
Anno gracie cxxiiij^{to} coronacio lucii.
Coronation dates of the kings from Lucius to Edward III., followed by brief annals (f. 14 *b*—f. 17) which are repeated for the most part at f. 32.
This first copy ends:
A. gr. m⁰. cccc⁰. xxvi^{to} in monasterio de Bermundesey obiit circa horas viii^{uam} et ix^{nam} de mane illustris principissa Regina Katerina filia francie dicti regis H. sexti genitrix et R. H. v^{ti} conthoralis.
Each copy has a rough sketch of the Royal arms as altered by Edw. III. (1338) in the margin (ff. 14*b*, 32).

On 17*b* is this entry: Fecit homagium henr. patri regis ut patet per huntyngdon apud Clar' hall.
On 18: filia Will^{mi} Marescalli prioris de cuius Will^i gestis insignibus tam pl'ibus quam militaribus licet in galica lingua insignis tamen composita est historia.
After f. 31 is a gap. The text breaks off in a note on the quinque Fulcones (R. de Diceto *Ymagines Historiarum,* Rolls Ser. II. 15).

A. d. m⁰. ccc⁰. xxvi^{to} coronacio Regis Edwardi tercii
A second copy of the annals given above (f. 14 *b*).
Ends (f. 35) with Hen. VI.: secundo Parisiis coronabatur post prius susceptam coronam Anglie apud Westm. etatis sue anno septimo. Cuius imperium Regni diu preseruet altissimus per tempora longiora. Amen.

5. Of the occupation of Winchester by monks, then canons,
   then monks again under Edgar and Dunstan . . . . f. 35 *b*
   Mem. quod per ccc. annos et amplius erant monachi in
   Wynton. ecclesia tempore britonum.
   Cf. Wharton, *Ang. Sac.* I. 217 sub fin.
   Notes on lawgivers : Moyses, Mercurius etc. . . . 38 *b*
   De uiris illustribus quo tempore scripserunt . . . 39
   Trogus Pompeius
   to Rad. de Diceto.
   From R. de Diceto, *Abbreviationes Chronicorum* (Rolls I. 20).
   Kings of Rome, Seven Wise Men, Twelve gods . . 42
   Nine worthies :
   Nouem valentes sunt qui pingi solent in aulis estiualibus
   uel in muris quorum tres sunt pagani etc.
   Hector, Alexander, Julius Caesar : Josue, Dauid,
   Machabeus : Arthurus, Karolus, Godofredus.
   De xv signis xv dierum precedencium diem iudicii . 43 *b*
   Ieronimus In annalibus hebreorum.

6. Statutes, viz.
   Magna Carta (confirmation by Edw. I.): ends imperfectly 44 *b*
   Carta de foresta (mut. init.) 52
   Prouisiones de Merton 56
   Stat. de Marleberga . . . . 60 *b*
   Westm. II. . . . . 69 *b*
   Quia emptores 106
   De Mercatoribus 107
   De Religiosis 108
   De finibus 109
   De presentibus vocatis ad warantum . . . . 111 *b*
   De vasto facto tempore alieno . . . . . 112 *b*
   De Bigamis . . . . 113 *b*
   De articulis in quibus non habet locum prohibicio . 115
   Regia prohibicio . . . . 115 *b*
   De admissis ad defencionem sui iuris . . . . 116 *b*
   De coniunctim feoffatis . . . . 117 *b*
   De conspiratoribus *et quia gallicum est ideo omitto* . 119 *b*
   De quo warranto III 120
   Capitula 121
   On the last leaf are scribbles 128
   Tanti post primam tu suscipe iungis aristam
   Nomen scriptoris qui Christo plenus amoris.
   and (later) Elley scriptoris qui plenus amoris
   Elizabeth Eloghe wiffe unto Robert Eloghe of Mynsterley,
   &c. . . . . 128 *b*

27. CHRONICA ETC.

Paper (and vellum), $8\frac{1}{4} \times 5\frac{5}{8}$, ff. 110, 34–36 lines to a page. Cent.
xv, irregularly written ; in a poor state.

Collation: 1 (two: vellum) 2^{12}–4^{12} 5^{14} (wants 13, 14) 6^{12} (wants 11, 12) 7^{12} (12 torn) one slip 8^{12} (wants 12) 9^{14} 10^{12} a^8 (blank).

1. [John Erghom's] commentary on certain metrical prophecies: addressed to Humphrey Bohun Earl of Hereford and Essex and Constable of England . . . . f. 1*b*

   Uenerabili domino et mira magnitudine extollendo... humfredo de Bowne Comiti Herford Essex Constabulario (*above line*: north) Angl. et domino de Breknok. dei gratia humilitatis suus si supra consequencie notam capud misericordie velitis adiungere nomen obscurum et obsequium salutar'.

   Lower part of page illegible.

   The author indicates his name, but very obscurely; it is Erghom. *Ergo* is "nota consequencie" and *m* is "caput misericordie." John Erghom was an Austin friar of York. His library is catalogued in a Dublin MS. (transcribed for me for publication) which contains the catalogue of the whole library of his house. He was evidently interested in occult and prophetic literature.

   This tract is printed by T. Wright, *Political Poems* (Rolls Series) I. 123.

ff. 3, 4 are mutilated.

Ends 31*b*: decet uenerari subleuantem. Expl. expositio huius prophecie.

2. These arn þe bages longing to þe Deuke of York: a list of his quarterings and their origin 31*b*
3. In double columns. Prophecies.

   Col. 1 headed De duracione 6^{ti}. Hybernie per Alanum.

   Col. 2 headed Ricardus Scrope Episcopus Ebor.

   Tertia lustra tenent serui cum tempora sexti

   ...sub quo dabit hic heremita (16 ll.).

   De etate 6^{ti} hybernie.

   Tolle caput martis bis cancri lumina fundat (32 ll.).

   Proverbs and scribbles.

   Wise men ben but scorned.

   This is the last song of Thomas of Arrledon (Ercildoune).

   114 lines in double columns.

   > When Rome is removed into Inglond
   > Each priest hath the popus power in hond.

   ...

   It shall be do within iij yeeres y wis.

   A text of this is printed in Lumby's *Bernardus* (E. E. T. S. 1870, p. 32).

   Distich. O rex si rex es rege te vel eris sine re rex

   nomen habes sine re te nisi recte regis.

4. De reventu regis Henrici VI^{ti} postquam coronatus erat

apud Parisium ad London   33
   Inter cetera nobilissimus ille prefectus cum discreto
   consilio
   —longitudine dierum adimplebo eum pro primo et
   ostendam illi salutare meum pro secundo.

5. De coronacione et unctione regis anglie . . .   34*b*
   Die quo consecrandus est dominus rex de nouo
   —officium pincernarie seruiet dominus comes de Arundell.

6. Mirabilia anglie secundum cronica Westm. . . .   37
   Ventus egreditur de cauernis terre in monte vocat' peke
   ...flumine que vocatur leum.

7. Another hand   39
   De iusticia regis Anglie ad Aquitaniam etc.
   Sciendum est quod anno domini 1136° Willelmus dux
   Aquitanie
   —et sic rex Anglie iuste et pacifice Walliam occupauit.
   Declaracio iusticie d. regis Anglie ad Regnum Scocie .   43
   A. d. 1301 papa Bonefacius
   —illibata persistere benignius permittatis.
   Notes on the age of the world, parentage of William I., and
   other historical notes, the last referring to 1307 . .   48
   On women—for and against, e.g.
   Quid est mulier. hominis confusio indesinens pugna etc.

8. De terra Iero(so)li(mi)tana   49
   Terra Ierosolimitana in centro mundi posita est ex maiori
   parte montuosa
   —sed ualde corrupte de diuersitate saracenorum et
   hostium christianitatis inferius dicetur.

9. Letters (2) of Pope Boniface and (3) of Edward I. concerning
   Ireland   52
   The last dated Lincoln 10 Feb. 1300.

10. Christian Kings of England : Alfred to Henry I. . .   61
    Ex rotulo Walsham fratris et doctoris Norwyci et primo
    de regibus etc.
    Other dates, e.g. of Charlemagne.
    Note on Bohemia. Bohemii intrauerunt Bas(ileam?) in
    quattuor turmis.

11. Maior proposicionis facte per M. Jo. Perin translata de
    gallico in latinum.   62
    Addressed to the Duke of Burgundy, dated 1407.
    Sequitur prima pars siue maior proposicionis etc.
    Penes nobilissimam et altissimam maiestatem regiam.
    There are passages in French, and many *exempla*.
    Ends 74*a* (*R.* half torn) : Sextum correlativum est quod
    omnis subiectus et vas(sallus).

12. Note on the Tower of Babel etc. : Iste nemroth erat gigas
    —ascanius suscepit regnum ita...

13. Chronicle from Brutus to 1366 . . . . . .   73 *b*
    Brutus post patris et matris interfeccionem
    —sic viagium compleuit in partibus Normaniis francie...

14. Verses on the kings : Alfred to Henry IV. (100 ll.) . .   80
    Alfredus rex Anglorum primusque monarcha
            ...
    Versibus bis centum lector tibi do documentum.

15. Quot regna erant in Anglia.
    Regnum Cancionum fuit in Cancia
        —et ex Eboraco fit archiepiscopatus similiter et
        Lichfield.
    De episcopatibus olim in Anglia.
    Anglia habet in longitudine octoginta miliaria.
    Scribbled notes : the Fall.

16. Prophecy. De sancta fide   82
    An. d. mil. ter. c. sex non sunt ista reperta.
    Classes diverse tendent ad prelia certa.
            ...
    Ista feras, te corde tegas, celestia pergas (44 ll.).

17. When the cock in the north hath bigged his nest
Ends : In Josaphat beried right shall he be.
    Cf. a text in Lumby's *Bernardus*, E. E. T. S.

18. Agreement in Star-chamber between Robert Prior of
    Norwich and ? The date 1523 occurs. The hand is of
    course later.

19. History of Richard I.
    Vicesima secunda die mensis Septembris Ricardus rex
    uenit messanam in sicilia.
    Includes the text of the Bull de libertatibus ecclesiarum
    Regni Scocie. Ends imperfectly, after an account of
    the diseases in the crusaders' camp.
        et responsum est ei ab uniuerso clero quod nullatenus.

28.   PETRUS BLESENSIS ETC. Pressmark N. 5. 181.

Vellum, $8\frac{1}{4} \times 5\frac{3}{4}$, ff. 95, 33–39 lines to a page : three volumes in one.
Cent. xiii, xiv, and xv.

Old skin binding with pads of parchment, cut from the cover of an
Infortiatum. This title in large letters is on the pad at the beginning.
On the 2nd cover an old title : Epistole petri.

On the flyleaf some receipts.

Collation : $1^8\ 2^6$, one slip, 3^8, one slip, $4^{10}\ 5^{12}$–$8^{12}\ 9^2\ 10^4$ (wants 4), one
slip, 11^8 (wants one).

I. Tractatus de fletu ecclesie (xiv—xv)   1
    Addressed to Urban VI.
    Begins imperfectly : ff. de minoribus b si filius et l.

Ends 13 b : emendacioni prefati sanctissimi patris et
prefatorum dominorum cardinalium. et sic explicatur
tractatus de fletu ecclesie.

Colophon in red : Eructans uere deus alme mei miserere.

II.   Petri Blesensis Epistolae CI   14
The first quire with *Tabula* and Epp. 1-4 (part) is of
cent. xiv–xv.

At top of the first of the older leaves (xiii) is : folium 400
Epistola 3.

The first Epistle is :
Conquestio regine anglorum super captionem regis et
filii sui Reuerendo domino et patri celestino.

The last Ep. 102 (101) (qui dabit capiti meo) ends
imperfectly, decebat ab iniuriis . . . .   87 b

III. Indulgences of Churches in Rome, cent. xv . . .   88
Sanctus silvester papa scribit in cronica sua quod rome
fuerunt mille quingenti quinque ecclesie.

Ends : diebus dominicis et veneris totius anni. Expl.
indulgentie vii ecclesiarum rome cum reliqui(i)s suis.

On the verso of the last page is a scribbled entry to the effect that
Simon Aylward "sub abbate de Bello loco in archidiaconatu Wynton."
(= Beaulieu in Hampshire) collector of tithe has received certain tithe
from the Rector of Bedhampton (10 Aug. 1487).

29.   IOH. FLETE.

Vellum, 10¼ × 7⅜, ff. 58, 32 lines to a page.   Cent. xv.
Collation: 1² (blank) 2⁸–8⁸.

In large letters on the flyleaf :

Iohannis Fleete Monachus West.

Contents :

J. Flete de fundatione ecclesie Westmonasteriensis.

On ff. 54, 55 is written a Bull of Julius II., 30 May 1504,
granting an Indulgence in respect of K. Henry VIIth's
new Lady Chapel.

On f. 55 b is a short extract from Walsingham's Hypo-
deigma Neustriae.

The text, which has never been printed *in extenso*, is being prepared
for publication by the Dean of Westminster.

30.   AELFRIC'S GRAMMAR.

Paper, small 4to, ff. 51 written, 28 lines to a page.   Cent. xvi.
Vellum wrapper.

On flyleaf:

Guilhelmi Lambardi ex dono Laurentij Noelli, 1565.

ꝶille hám lampyrhte.

Ic Aelfric ꝶold þas lytlan boc aꝶendan to engliscum gereorde

errorem corrigere

—gif he nele his þoh gerihtan.

The Anglo-Saxon alphabet is written below.

Vox est aer ictus sensibilis

Stema is geslagen lyft.

Ends: on eallum dagum 7 us dyrne ꝶævon.   Si þis boc þúss her geendod.   Finit.

on leden spræce synd menig fealde getele

— 7 þrittig penegas ænne mancus.

Nomina multarum rerum anglice.

Dominus þæt is god ælmihtig

...

pila pilestocc oþþe þoþer loquela.

Edited by Zupitza.

31.   POEMS TO QUEEN ELIZABETH.

Paper, $7\frac{3}{4} \times 5\frac{3}{4}$, ff. 84, 16 lines to a page.   Cent. xvi.

Very well written.   Initials in red.   At the top of p. 1 the name Ward, which is repeated on the last page.   Also on the last page George Merrill (or perhaps Meryill) partially erased.

Purchased 15 July, 1846 for £7 (Chapter order).

Collation: 1^4 2^8 3^{14} 4^{14} 5^8 6^8 7^{12} (last one missing) 8^{12} (last one missing) 9^6.   Inside the cover is a letter from H. H. Edwards, dated July 13th 1836, giving information about the recent history of the book.

Contents:

One of the poems is dated 1587.   A few are in Greek.

The following authors' signatures appear.

Richard Ireland	f.	4 *b.*
Peter Smart		11 *b.*
Henry Child		19 *b.*
Roger Derham		24 *b.*
William Driwood		29 *b.*
John Matthew		33 *b.*
Charles Pratt		40 *a.*
Richard Marche		49 *b.*
John Packer		55 *b.*
John Whitgift		59 *b.*
Jasper Swift		60 *b.*
Hugo Roberts		67 *b.*
Walter Newton		70 *b.*
William Boil		74 *b.*
Thomas Owen		78 *b.*
Richard Johnson		82 *b.*

On verso of last page—

> "Nunc opus exegi quod nec Jovis ira nec ignis
> Nec poterit ferrum nec edax abolere vetustas."

32.　　　　　COMPENDIUM METAPHYSICAE.

Paper, 12ᵐᵒ, ff. cir. 80: minute writing.　Cent. xvii, early.

Compendium Metaphysicae in quo succincta Methodus et ordo Suarez probe obseruatur.

Given in 1725 by Dr Only.　See Register.

33.　　　　　CONTROVERSIAE.

Paper, 12ᵐᵒ, ff. circa 300.　Cent. xvi–xvii, well written.

Controversiae nostri temporis in Epitomen redactae.

Ex dono Joh. Jones alumni Reg. 1705.

34.　　　　　FRAGMENTS.

1.　Vellum, 8 × 5⅝, ff. ·2, double columns of 35 lines.　Cent. xiii.

Fragment of Trotula de curis egritudinum mulierum.

2.　Paper, 11¾ × 8¾, ff. 6.　Cent. xv.

Fragment of treatise on Canon Law.

3.　Vellum, 10½ × 7⅜, ff. 46, 25 lines to a page.　Cent. xiii.

Marked 19. 20.

Collation: 1¹²–3¹² 4¹⁰ (one mutilated).

Quoniam in ante expositis libris de partibus orationis.

f. 37 b: Expl. liber primus parcinus (?) et post inc. secundus...
Scriptor in studio sudat peccunie lucro
Lepos scribendi si (sed ?) raro veniunt nummi.

Ends: quorum actus ad res carentes loquela pertinent primas qui et secundas.

4.　Vellum, 9½ × 7⅝, ff. 12, double columns of 42 lines.　Cent. xiii.

Comment on Gen. i. x.

5.　Paper, 11½ × 8½, ff. 25, 62 lines to a page.　Cent. xv, on vellum wrapper.

Collation: 1¹² (wants 1) 2¹⁴.

Omne quod incipit esse
—que est ipsius materia.

6. Paper, $11\frac{1}{2} \times 8\frac{1}{2}$, ff. 12, double columns of 62–68 lines. Cent. xv.

Fragments of the Topica of Aristotle.

7. Paper, $11\frac{5}{8} \times 8\frac{1}{4}$, ff. 23, 47–57 lines to a page. Cent. xv.

Fragment of a medical treatise (five chapters).
The last section is : Cap. nonum de apoplexia.

8. Vellum, $11 \times 7\frac{3}{8}$, f. 1.

Leaf of a gloss on Psalms (xcvii. xcviii.) : there is one large initial.

9. Paper, $11\frac{1}{4} \times 8\frac{1}{4}$, ff. 16, 30–32 lines to a page. Cent. xv.

Fragment of Chronicles of Normandy (?) in French, dealing with Robert of Normandy.

10. Vellum, $13 \times 9\frac{5}{8}$, ff. 4, 21 lines to a page. Cent. xv, in fine Italian hand.

Fragment of a Law-book.

11. Vellum, $6 \times 4\frac{1}{4}$, ff. 6. Cent. xiv (?).

Part of Latin-English vocabulary : followed by some French.

12. Vellum, $9\frac{1}{2} \times 6\frac{1}{4}$, ff. 1 and fragment. Cent. xv (?).

Index of a Law-book.

13. Paper, $8\frac{3}{4} \times 5\frac{3}{4}$, ff. 16, 23 lines to a page. Cent. xv.

Fragment of the Organon of Aristotle (?).

14. Paper, $8\frac{5}{8} \times 5\frac{3}{4}$, ff. 6.

French ballads.

15. Vellum, $6\frac{7}{8} \times 4\frac{1}{2}$, ff. 9. Cent. xiii, very fragmentary.

16. Vellum, $5\frac{5}{8} \times 3\frac{3}{4}$, f. 1. Cent. xiii.

17. Vellum, 8×7, f. 1 (fragmentary). Cent. xiii—xiv.

Fragment of Sermon-book.

18. Paper, $7\frac{1}{2} \times 5\frac{1}{2}$, f. 1. Cent. xvi.

Fragment of a petition to Queen Elizabeth.

V.

DESCRIPTIONS OF THE WESTMINSTER CHARTULARIES.

I. *Munim. Bk* 11, Domesday.'

A large folio, parchment, ff. 1—685, written at the beginning of the 14th century. The latest document of the original compilation appears to be the Disclaimer of the Bp of Winchester to the effect that he does not intend to infringe the privileges of the Abbey by his coming to crown K. Edward II, dated 6 Mar. 1308 (f. 675). Many later documents have been subsequently inserted (one dated 1445).

A leaf is lost before f. 1; another between ff. 409 and 410. A gathering of 8 leaves has been displaced, so that ff. 492—499 now stand after f. 508.

This great Chartulary came to be known as 'Domesday.' It is referred to under this title in Dean Goodman's time (*Munim.* 1,808 and 1,874). The name is possibly due to the later extracts from the Domesday Book on ff. 29 b seqq., where the word occurs. as a headline: on the other hand it may be remembered that St Paul's also has its 'Domesday[1].'

The chief contents are:

f. 1. Papal bulls, from Innocent II to Boniface VIII (the latest, 1299).

f. 29 b. [Extracts from Domesday—in a later hand.]

f. 35. Charters of St Dunstan, Edgar, St Edward, etc. to Edward III [and, in a later hand, to Henry VI].

f. 79. Evidences of Estates, arranged by counties.

f. 349. Scripta Prioratus.

f. 360. „ Cantoris.

f. 363. „ Sacristae.

---

[1] Also there is a 'Domesday Book of Felley Priory' [co. Nottingham ; Augustinian], Brit. Mus. Add. MS. 36,872.

f. 410.   Sacristae Indulgentiae.
f. 433.   Anniversary of Q. Eleanor.
f. 465.   Scripta Celerarii.
f. 471.   „   Hostillarii Forinseci.
f. 479 *b*.   „   „   Intrinseci.
f. 480 *b*.   „   Refectorarii.
f. 482.   „   Elemosinariae.
f. 495.   „   Camerarii.
f. 532 *b*.   „   Capellae Beatae Mariae.
f. 596 *b*.   „   Infirmarii.
f. 610 *b*.   „   Coquinarii.
f. 621.   „   Pitanciarii.
f. 647 *b*.   „   Gardinarii.
f. 656.   Literae Pensionariae Communes (Churches with their pensions in London diocese).
f. 659.   Compositiones (chiefly between the Abbot aud the Monks).
f. 671.   Confederationes (alliances with other monasteries).
f. 674.   Literae Testimoniales Privilegiorum (Protests and Disclaimers).
f. 678.   Scripta vacua nunc.

There are about 20 notes written in the margins by a bold hand of the middle of the 15th century, to indicate that certain supplementary documents are to be sought in the 'Black Paper Register.' The following are specimens:

f. 37.   Forma Juramenti confugiencium ad Sanctuarium Westm' queras in nouo Registro Nigri paperi.

f. 75 *b*.   Carta Regis Ricardi secundi de quodam uestimento aurotexto per eundem dato ecclesie Westm' quere in registro nigro paperi Westm'. Item ibidem de quodam anulo aureo cum i ruby pretiosissimo dato per eundem ecclesie Westm', quem postea dn̄s rex Henricus iiii habuit in custodia.

f. 594.   Indentura...queratur in registro Nigri paperi Westm', et similiter in registro officii capelle beate Marie, In quo registro omnia seriatim scribuntur tam carte quam Firme terre et tenementorum eidem remanentium usque ad annum quartum r. r. Henrici quarti.

The documents thus referred to are now to be found in the third section of the *Liber Niger Quaternus*, which thus seems to be a copy on parchment of the paper Black Book.

II. *Munim. Bk* 12.

A large folio, parchment, ff. 1—214; the original hand is of the early part of the 15th century; illuminated borders and initials.

The chief contents are:

ff. 1—25.   An Index to Papal bulls and a few other instruments contained in the *prima cista*. They extend as far as Urban VI, but do not include (save as a later insertion) Boniface IX who succeeded him in 1389. They are indexed alphabetically, both under Popes and under subjects.

ff. 26—30 are blank.

ff. 31—87. The documents of the contest with the Dean and College of Sᵗ Stephen's Chapel in the Palace ; with a table of contents prefixed. They extend from the Citation of the Dean, 31 Jan. 1377, to the final Composition, 10 Aug. 1394, and its confirmation by K. Richard II. The oaths of Canons and Vicars are recorded as far as Jan. 1409.

ff. 88—108 were originally left blank. They contain in later hands

(1) Documents relating to the visitation of the Hospital of St James (89—94);

(2) to the appropriations of Langedon (95*b*—100*a*), Mordon (100*b*—101*b*), Aldenham (101*b*—106*b*).

ff. 109—114. A Commission in Edward II's reign, before which the Abbot was summoned to declare *Quo Warranto* he held his manors of Westerham, &c.

ff. 115, 116, originally left blank, now contain 'Mensuracio terrae in com : Hertford' (a 16th cent. heading): *inc.* 'Tria grana ordei faciunt unum pollicem.'

ff. 117—200. Evidences of various estates, partly in a contemporary hand and partly in later hands.

ff. 201—207 are blank.

ff. 208—212*a*. A Terrier of the Manor of Westbury, Co. Wilts, with names of fields and persons : in a later hand.

ff. 212*b*—214 are blank.

N.B. The splendid collection of Papal bulls and other Papal instruments to the number of 208, ranging from Paschal II (1099—1118) to Urban VI (1378—1389)[1], had disappeared already in 1537. For there are still preserved (*Munim.* lviii) some loose paper pages entitled ' A book of the benefyces impropered to the monastorye of Westʳ, remayning in the custodye of Jhon Gemme, and in the Thresurye, aᵒ xxixᵒ Henrici viii.' The writer gives such information as he can as to documents concerning Appropriations still to be found (5 Sept. 1537), apparently with a view of discovering which were made by Papal bulls. The bulls themselves were no longer there to be consulted, and he speaks more than once of ' illa cista ubi bulle papales erant.'

III. *Munim. Bk* 1, 'Liber Niger Quaternus.'

A large quarto, parchment, ff. 1—151, besides 8 leaves unnumbered at the beginning : written towards the end of the 15th century.

The chief contents are :

ff. (1)—(8). 'Tabula tocius illius libri.'

ff. 1—76. [*Liber Primus.*] Documents relating to properties in Westminster, Eye, Stanes, Iveney, Lalham, Denham, Pyrford, Pershore, Deerhurst, Sutton, Islip. These documents fall into two classes according to their dates : (1) copies

---

[1] Besides one of Boniface IX added to the Index by a later hand.

of documents (and often merely of a series of headings) from Bk 12, the Westminster 'Domesday,' (2) similar documents of the 14th and 15th centuries, the last on f. 76 being dated 1408.

ff. 76 *b*—93. *Secundus Liber*. A collection of memoranda of the most diverse kinds. At the end (f. 93) is an index ('Tabula istius secundi libri'), running from f. i to f. ix : its items correspond nearly but not quite to those which are in the present book, ff. 76—81. On ff. 81—92 are many brief notes of historical interest, as well as several documents relating to General Chapters of the Benedictines.

ff. 93 *b*—151. *Tertius Liber*. Documents of various kinds, many of which are briefly summarised in the preceding book of memoranda : e.g. Westminster fairs (93 *b*), property of Nicholas Brembre (97), Benedictine College at Oxford (97 *b*), agreements for anniversaries (99 *b*, &c.), tenements in Westminster (100 *b*—117), Chapel of St Stephen (118—124), nuns of Kilburn (125), properties in Westminster (127 *b*—133), St James's Hospital (137), Oaths of sanctuarymen (139 *b*), Monastic offices and their incomes (140), Sheriffs of Worcester (144), Memoranda from accounts of officials (145), Cardinal Simon Langham's legacy (146 *b*—150).

The documents, about 35 in number, which are referred to in the marginal notes of *Munim. Bk* 11, are all to be found in the *Tertius Liber*, with four exceptions: (1) the gift of a Vestment by K. Rich. II, (2) the indenture as to books lent to Thomas Southam, Archdeacon of Oxford, (3) 'Redditus et servitia diversorum maneriorum annuatim ad auditum compoti deferendi,' (4) 'Modus respondendi de exitu diversorum animalium.' The first two of these are summarised, but not transcribed, in the memoranda contained in the *Secundus Liber* (ff. 86, 79).

We may accordingly conclude that the 'New Black Paper Register,' quoted in the margins of Bk 11, is now represented (though not quite in its original completeness) by the third section of *Liber Niger Quaternus*.

The following memoranda in the *Secundus Liber* throw some light on this Paper Register:

1. In the Tabula on f. 93 we find the heading: 'Notule diuerse in Nigro papiro Rogeri Kyrton.' When we turn back to the place referred to we find a series of headings of matters which it is said will be given below—'postea folio...'; but the reference is not filled in. As a matter of fact the items occur in full in the *Tertius Liber*.

2. In the same Tabula is the heading : 'De euidenciis Mulsam Bekeswell etc. in Nigro papiro.' This is not to be found in its place on f. 79 : but it comes later (f. 81), and runs as follows : '*De euidenciis de Mulsham in papiro Creton*. Mem^d quod in papiro Rogeri Cretton sunt euidencie clare de Mulseham Bekeswell Westerham Wendelsworth et aliis, que deberent Registrari in Nouo Registro, et parcelle optime habentur in dicto papiro que non sunt alibi in promptu iam reperte. Et ideo fiat prouidentia de Scriptori etc.'

We may therefore assign the Black Paper Register to Roger Cretton (or Kyrton), who was Treasurer c. 1408—1411. We learn from the

Infirmarer's roll that he sang his first mass in 1387–8, and from the Chamberlain's roll that he was still living in 1430.

The following notes from the beginning of *Liber Niger Quaternus* itself tell the subsequent history:

1. At the end of the *Tabula totius libri*:

> Quem nigrum veteres quondam dixere quaternum
> Me Thomas Clyfford composuit monachus.

2. The rubricated title on f. 1:

Liber quaternus niger ex antiquo denominatus, quem Thomas dns Clifforde vir honorabilis ac huius monasterii beati Petri Westm. quondam monachus ad suos sumptus expensasque fieri fecit de nouo in tempore Reverendissimi in Christo patris et dñi Dñi Johannis Estney permissione diuina prefati monasterii abbatis prestantissimi, in dei gloriam et perpetuam ecclesiastici iuris memoriam, feliciter incipit.

John Esteney was Abbot from 1474—1498. Thomas Clifford is first mentioned in the Chamberlain's roll of 1463–4: he is not in the roll of the previous year. We learn from the roll of the *Novum Opus* that he sang his first mass in 1466–7. In 1483 he exchanged the Wardenship of the Lady Chapel for the office of Treasurer which he held till Mich. 1484: the Treasurers' roll for the next year is missing[1]. His name does not appear in the Chamberlain's roll for 1484–5. He seems to have died in September 1485[2].

The style 'Thomas dns Clifforde vir honorabilis ac huius monasterii quondam monachus' is remarkable. He is not 'Dan Thomas Clifford,' but Thomas Lord Clifford' apparently: though the word 'dns' is, as a matter of fact, written over the last letters of 'Thomas,' as though it had at first been omitted. Moreover he is described as 'honorabilis.'

Now the Clifford family had a somewhat romantic history at this period. Thomas de Clifford, Lord Clifford, was slain at St Albans in 1455. His son John Clifford, called the Butcher,' fought against the Yorkists at Wakefield in 1460, and fell at Ferrybridge in 1461: he was attainted and his estates were forfeited. Henry, his eldest son, was brought up as a shepherd to elude observation: he was restored to his titles and estates in 1485.

---

[1] There are no Treasurers' rolls for 1484–5, 1485–6. But there is a 'visus computi' of John Hampton, Treasurer, Bailiff, and Warden of the Churches, for all moneys received by him 'immediate post decessum fratris Thomae Clifford, qui non computavit nuper Thes. Ball. Custod. eccl. super auditum computorum praedictorum determinatum ad festum S. Mich. aº Hen. VII. 1º.'

[2] The item 'pro anima T. Clifford' in the Infirmarer's roll indicates that he was dead before Mich. 1485; but the roll of the Warden of K. Henry Vth's manors shews him still making some of the payments for that king's anniversary (31 Aug.).

The genealogy in Whitaker's *History of Craven* gives 'Thomas *d.s.p.*' as fifth child of Thomas Lord Clifford, whose first child John was born in 1435. It seems then that 'Thomas dñs Clifford' was a younger brother of the attainted baron, and uncle of the 'Shepherd Lord'; that he found shelter as a monk at Westminster in the troubles which followed the accession of K. Edward IV, and that he died almost immediately after K. Henry VIIth's accession (22 Aug.), which restored the fortunes of his family.

IV. *Munim. Bk* 3.

A large folio, parchment, pp. 1—94: somewhat mutilated, and with several leaves bound in wrong order. Entitled in large black letters on p. 3: 'In isto Libello facto Tempore Reverendissimi in cristo patris Bone memórie Johĩs Yslip tunc Abbatis. Ex sumptibus Fratris Thome Jay quondam Thesaurarii Monasterii Sancti Petri Westmonasterii Continentur appropriaciones diuersarum Ecclesiarum cum earum pertinenciis dicto Monasterio appropriatarum quarum nomina modo Alphabetico sequuntur inferius.'

It contains a selection of documents relating to Appropriations, many of which are found elsewhere. At the end two leaves of a Psalter in a late hand are bound in.

Two books (or parts of books) are here bound up together, each containing Appropriations in alphabetical order. The first (pp. 5—77) is rubricated, and of slightly smaller size than the second, which is not rubricated. Many documents appear twice over.

Thomas Jay was treasurer from 1514 to 1528, when he became prior.

V. British Museum, Cotton MS., *Faustina* A iii.

Parchment, a small thick volume, 356 ff.

ff. 2 *b*, 3. Pro herc' henrici .iii. ccc. Marc'. &c.
> Similar notes for Q. Eleanor, Q. Philippa, Edw. III, Q. Anne, Bp of Sarum, Bernard Brokas Miles, 'Rich. per dominum Regem Henr. V,' Hen. V, 'Domini le Bowser.'

f. 4. Incipiunt capitula libri cartarum a Regibus Anglie Westmonaster' ecclesie concessarum una cum explanacione de eiusdem loci construccione.

f. 11. Hic incipit prologus de...
> Venerabili...[=Sulcard].

f. 17. Regnanti...[=Edgar's Great Charter].

ff. 149—210. Papal bulls, ending with Statute of Ottobon.

f. 218. Inc. capitula libri compositionum, confederationum, &c.

f. 354. Letter of John abbot of Westm. to prior of the House or Cell of Gt Malvern (Visitation).
> At the end are scribbled the names of John Denys and Rich. Stone.

[John Denys was 'custos bosci de Estgrove,' 1461-88 : and in Jan. 1497 John Denys 'surgeon barbour' had a lease of a garden in the almonry. Richard Stone, 'gentilman,' was 'parcarius de Denham' in 1487 : he first appears in the service of the Abbey in 1472 : he held many leases, and died about 1511.]

So many hands have worked on this book that I invoked the aid of Dr G. F. Warner, who most kindly tabulated them for me as follows:

1. ff. 2*b*, 3. Mid. 15th cent.
2. ff. 4—9*b* (Capitula). Early 14th cent.
3. ff. 9*b*, 1. 16—10*b* (Capit.). 15th cent.
4. ff. 11—16*b*. Late 13th cent.
5. ff. 17—113. Late 13th cent. (different from 4).
6. ff. 113*b*, last two lines—142*b*. 15th cent. (partly same hand as 3).
7. ff. 143—148. Later 15th cent. additions.
8. ff. 149—153*b* (Capit.). Same hand as 2.
9. ff. 154, 155 (Capit.). Same hand as 3.
10. ff. 156*b*. Early 14th cent.
11. ff. 157—193. Early 14th cent.
12. ff. 193*b*—204. Same hand as 6.
13. ff. 216, 217. Late 15th cent.
14. ff. 218—222 (Capit.). Same hand as 2.
15. ff. 223, 224. Same hand as 3.
16. ff. 225—258. Same hand as 11.
17. ff. 258*b*—259*b*. 15th cent. (partly same hand as 12).
18. ff. 260—291. Same hand as 16.
19. ff. 291, 1. 9—347. Same hand as 12.
20. ff. 347*b*—end. Various later additions (last date 1511).

Practically four stages in the composition of the MS.

1st. Nos. 4, 5.
2nd. Nos. 2, 8, 10, 11, 14, 16, 18.
3rd. Nos. 3, 6, 9, 12, 15, 17, 19.
4th. Remainder.

The history of the book then may be briefly described thus. Its earliest element is:

1. Sulcard 'de constructione,' &c. followed by Royal Charters [two hands of late xiiith cent.].

Then towards the end of Edw. I's reign were added:

2. Papal Bulls.
3. Compositions, Confederations, &c.
Also *capitula* for the three sections in a different hand.

In the xvth cent. considerable additions were made to each of the three sections, and *capitula* to correspond were added in yet another hand.

Thus the book corresponds generally to parts of ' Domesday ' :

1. Royal Charters (= D. ff. 35—78).
2. Papal Bulls (= D. ff. 1—34).
3. Compositions, &c. (= D. ff. 659—674).

But ' Domesday ' is an immense volume and contains besides :

Evidences of Estates, arranged by counties (ff. 79—348).

Evidences belonging to various Obedientiaries (ff. 349—656).

With a view to the investigation of the relation between the two books the following notes from *Faust.* A iii may be recorded here.

f. 149.　*Incipiunt Capitula privilegiorum ecclesie scī Petri Westm'.*
　　　Nicholaus et Leo suscipiunt ecclesiam beati Petri Westmon' sub protectione sedis apostolice : set hec duo Privilegia remanent in custodia dn̄i Regis : quorum note reperiri poterunt in primis cartis sancti Regis Edwardi. [These are imaginary bulls, cited in the forged charters of the Confessor.]
　　　Capitulum i. Paschal. ii.　Paschalis papa ii°.......*Innocentius ii. Cap^m ii.* ......*C^m iii.* Idem precipit Abbati Gervasio......*Cap^m Quartum.* Idem perhibet testimonium quod ecclesia Westm' a tempore......*Capitulum v°.* Idem confirmat.......

After the Index two pages blank ; then

f. 156 *b.*　*Protectio dn̄i Regis contra infestatores.*
　　　Innocencius episcopus, servus servorum Dn̄i, karissimo in Christo filio Henrico.
　　　With a rubric in the margin : ' Ista bulla debet registrari in ii° folio sequenti.'

It will be seen by reference to Dr Warner's table that this bull is copied by a different hand from that which writes the Index and also from that which writes the bulls which follow. It had been accidentally omitted. An attempt was made to straighten matters by adding numbers in the margin, thus :

			[marg.]	
f. 157.　Paschal II . 　.　.　.　.　.　.　.　.				i
f. 158.　Innoc. II to Gervase 　.　.　.　.　.			,,	iiii
f. 159.　　,,　　to Gervase and monks　.　.　.			,,	iii

It is to be noted that there is a somewhat similar confusion, and a somewhat similar note, at the same point in ' Domesday.'

VI.　British Museum, Cotton MS., *Titus* A viii.

Parchment, about 8 in. by 6 in., ff. 1—145. The first part of the volume, ff. 1—64, is, with small exceptions, in a neat hand of xivth cent. The second part, ff. 65—145, is a distinct book in a xiiith cent. hand : it has an ancient press-mark (S. 153) and on f. 145 *b*, ' Per Willm̄ Heyhom. Amen.' This portion belonged to Bury St Edmund's.

Two blank ff.

f. 1. 'Catalogus Tractatuum in isto volumine' (xviith cent.).

f. 2. '*Hic incipit prologus de prima constr*'. &c. (Sulcard, apparently copied from *Faustina* A iii).

f. 5 *b*. Edgar's Great Charter.

f. 7. Dunstan's.

ff. 9—11 *b*. First, Second and Third of Edward.

ff. 14 *b*—30 *b*. William I (four long and several short charters) and other kings.

f. 30 *b*. A long French charter of Edw. I, on Q. Eleanor's manors.

ff. 32, 33. On St James's Hospital (xvth cent.).

ff. 34—44. Compositions (including Stephen Langton's).

ff. 45—53. Papal Grants.

ff. 54 ff. Confederations, &c.

f. 59 *b*. 'Inprimis custodes fer' intrabunt civitatem Winton.' Rules for Winchester fair, to which the Westminster fair was assimilated.

ff. 61 *b*—64 *b*. General charter of Hen. III ('Anglicana ecclesia libera sit,' &c.).

[This ends the xivth cent. book.]

f. 65. '*Incipit epistola passionis Sc̄i Aedmundi premissa*,' &c. (Abbo to Dunstan).

f. 110. '*Incipit* [then, in a xvith cent. hand, over an erasure : 'epistola Osberti de Clara prioris Westm.']. In exodo legitur,' &c. (Miracles of St Edmund).

VII. [Not now to be traced : known from the following description.]

London : Printed by Samuel Bentley, Dorset St., Fleet Street.

Title : 'Abstract of Charters and other documents contained in a Cartulary of the Abbey of St Peter, Westminster, in the possession of Samuel Bentley. Printed for Private Circulation, 1836.' 76 pp., octavo.

This Chartulary seems to have been a copy, with modifications, of *Liber Niger Quaternus*: like that it is distributed into [*Liber Primus*], *Liber Secundus* and *Liber Tertius*: and the contents generally are the same.

It is probably the book referred to by Widmore in his manuscript Catalogue of the Muniments (p. 3) as 'in the custody of the Widow of Mr Spiller Reynolds of Sheperton. N.B. This is a Duplicate or Transcript of the *Niger Quaternus*.'

It is probable also that the same book is referred to in Stanley, *Memorials of Westminster*, ed. 3, app. iv, p. 640 [this appendix is omitted from later editions] :

(From a Cartulary of Westminster in the possession of Sir Charles G. Young, Garter King at Arms.)

Sequitur de renovatoribus, &c.

This is found in *Liber Niger Quaternus*, f. 92*b*; but as here given it is considerably enlarged and brought up to date. In Bentley's Chartulary the same document occurs:

432. De renovatoribus et benefactoribus capellarum in circuitu infra ecclesiam Mon. Westm. . . . . **f. xcvii**

VIII. Cambridge, *University Library*, Kk. 5. 29. 'Extenta Maneriorum.' One of Bp Moore's books.

Parchment, 10½ in. by 7 in., ff. 1—131. The original book begins at f. 21, with Todyngton (the first portion of which is missing).

ff. 1—11 ; xv, middle. 'Campus Australis de Holme.
Territorium de Holme, Langford, Clifton, Henlowe, Bikeleswade, Southynelle et le Brome, factum tempore fratris Johannis Flete, custodis maneriorum Regum et Reginarum,' etc.
f. 12 is lost.
f. 13, originally blank, now filled with scribblings ; e.g. :

> In te domine speravi } Thomas Jay.
> To Joy in god apply thy mind}
>
> Memorandum to speke for to mend the bordes in the burgon bytwix master Stanley and me &c.
> Jħus esto michi Jhesus Amen.
> Jħs est amor meus.

f. 14, col. 1. Custum' de Todyngton.
> Custum' de Echelesford.
> etc. etc.

[A table of contents including also Hampsted, Knyghtebrygge, Mordon, Batriches', Hendon, Aldenham, Whethamsted, Kenesbourne, Stevenach, Asshewell, Feryng, Kelveden, Southbemflet, Fanton.]

col. 2. Mensuracio terre de Greneford.

[Also Halughford, Combe, Downe, (and in another hand) Stratford att bowe.]
Several documents follow : one of 1454 : another (f. 16) from Records, 49 Edw. III.
f. 21. Todyngton [Extenta maneriorum]. xiv early.
f. 120*a*. 'Extenta' ends with Fanton.
A few later documents follow to the end of the book (f. 131).

The Hampstead portion of this book ('coram fratre Johanne de Buterleye,' 7 Nov. 1312) has been printed by Mr James Kennedy, *Manor and Parish Church of Hampstead* (1906).

ADDENDUM

In Messrs Floyer and Hamilton's Catalogue of the Manuscripts in the Library of Worcester Cathedral (p. 172) is printed an extract from the Chapter-books which throws an interesting light upon the pains taken by Dean Williams to enrich his newly-founded Library at Westminster. It appears from this document that he obtained letters under the Great Seal authorizing him to apply to the Chapter of Worcester Cathedral (and perhaps to other Chapters) for the grant of such manuscripts as they considered to be duplicates. It may be remembered that Sir Thomas Bodley not many years before had obtained (through his brother George, who was a member of the body) a large gift of manuscripts from the Chapter of Exeter. Very probably this fact was in Williams's mind when he made his application to Worcester.

The application, as we see, was favourably received, and twenty manuscripts were selected and sent up to London to the Dean. But I must regard it as extremely doubtful whether they ever arrived at the Library. It is true that some of the titles of the commoner books do occur in one or other of the Westminster lists, but the majority are not to be found there. Of the first four in the Worcester list, No. 1 occurs in List A (91) but not in Williams's own list (B): Nos. 2, 3, 4 are not to be found. Nos. 6, 7, 11, 13, possibly 19, and 20 correspond to entries in the Westminster lists, but these are all of the commonest sort: and for the others no certain equivalent is discoverable. What became of the books remains a mystery. It is possible that some may have been returned to Worcester.

A full copy of the entry in the Worcester chapter-book, which we owe to the kindness of the Ven. J. M. Wilson, Canon of Worcester, is subjoined.

At a Chapter held 3rd February, 1624.

Whereas letters from his Majesty directed unto us under the great Seal of England for all such dubble maniscripts as we have dubble in our library towards the furnishing of a Library in the Church of Westminster newly erected or augmented by the new Lord keeper. Wherupon we consented as by our Chapter Act bearing the 25th day of November 1623 doth appear. Now we whose names are subscribed by virtue of the said letters and consent of the Dean and Chapter and as by a letter from Mr Dean unto us of the chapter bearing date the 22d of January 1624 have sent up the said maniscripts unto Mr Dean to London for the better conveying thereof and to the said purpose appointed, viz. :

1. Augustinus de Ci*vitate* Dei.
2. Idem de verbis Domini [F. 32][1].
3. Anselmi varia.
4. Gregorii Pastorale.
5. Prophetæ 12 cum glossa [Q. 8].
6. Psalterium cum glossa [F. 47].
7. Pauli Epistolæ cum glossa [F. 49].
8. Historia Scholastica [F. 1 etc.].
9. Vocabularium Bibliorum Huberti (*or* Imberti) monachi cui titulus Prometheus [also in F. 1].
10. Sermones Jacobi de Losanna de sanctis [Q. 19. 2].
11. Magister sententiarum [F. 2, F. 98 etc.].
12. Determinationes quolibetorum Henrici de Gandano(-uo) [F. 79].
13. Digessum (-tum) novum [F. 136].
14. Innocentius in Decretalia (*or* es) [F. 170].
15. Decretales cum glossa [F. 59 etc.].
16. Concordantia discordantium canonum [F. 120].
17. Breviarium Extravagantiu*m* Bernardi Papiensis [F. 122].
18. Legenda S[torum] Jacobi Januensis [F. 45].
19. Brito vocabularius [F. 13].
20. Prisciani Grammatica.

RIC$\overline{\text{US}}$ POTTER, *Subdecanus.*
W. BARKESDALE, *Receiver.*
HENRY BRIGHT.

[1] The letters and numbers in brackets are the press-marks of manuscripts still at Worcester which correspond to entries in the list.

(M. R. J.)

ADDENDA ET CORRIGENDA.

p. 1. In view of Mr Edmund Bishop's note on p. 63 of the 'Bosworth Psalter,' I must modify the statement that Lanfranc's Constitutions were drawn up for all Benedictine monasteries in England. They were intended, as his preface shews, for Christ Church, Canterbury : they were introduced at St Albans by his nephew Paul ; and probably they were drafted with a view to the wider circulation which they afterwards had.

p. 9, l. 19. *For* 1486 *read* 1386. Some interesting changes seem indicated by the following notes from the rolls of the Wardens of Q. Eleanor's manors : 1454-5 (J. Flete and J. Esteney) 'et sic debet adhuc lxiii[s] viii[d]   Que quidem summa condonatur eidem pro reparacione librorum et renovacione in Nova libraria' : 1457-8, 'et eidem vi[s] viii[d] pro T. Myllyng pro labore suo in compilacione unius tabule in libraria.'

p. 11. An earlier mention of Seyny books occurs in the Q. Eleanor roll for 1465-6 : postea allocatur eidem [*sc.* W. Chertesey] xxv[s] v[d] q[a] pro Reparacione librorum vocatorum le seyny bokys.'

p. 22, l. 22. In Boston's list the no. 11 stands against Ailred's *Life of St Edward*,· Gilbert's *Disputation of a Jew*, and Laurence's *Sermons.*

(J. A. R.)

INDEX I

OF EXISTING MANUSCRIPTS.

INDEX II

NAMES OF ABBOTS, MONKS AND OTHER PERSONS CONNECTED
WITH THE MONASTERY.

(The last class are in italics.)

CAMBRIDGE: PRINTED BY JOHN CLAY, M.A. AT THE UNIVERSITY PRESS.